THE ETHICS
OF ABORTION

Other Books in the At Issue Series:

THE ETHICS
OF ABORTION

Jennifer A. Hurley, *Book Editor*

David L. Bender, *Publisher*
Bruno Leone, *Executive Editor*
Bonnie Szumski, *Editorial Director*
Stuart B. Miller, *Managing Editor*

AT ISSUE

An Opposing Viewpoints® Series

Greenhaven Press, Inc.
San Diego, California

MAY - - 2004

CO

Library of Congress Cataloging-in-Publication Data

The ethics of abortion / Jennifer A. Hurley, book editor.
    p. cm.—(At issue)
    Includes bibliographical references and index.
    ISBN 0-7377-0469-1 (pbk. : alk. paper)—ISBN 0-7377-0470-5
    (lib. : alk. paper)
    1. Abortion—Moral and ethical aspects. I. Hurley, Jennifer A.,
    1973– II. At issue (San Diego, Calif.)

HQ767.15 .E83 2001
179.7'6—dc21

                                                              00-058716

Table of Contents

Introduction

The controversy over the ethics of abortion centers around the question of when human life begins. Abortion opponents, believing the fetus to be a human being from the moment of conception, regard abortion as murder. As the editors of *Christianity Today* write, "abortion is one of those monumental issues of justice that comes along once in a lifetime. It is violence against children, a hideous act of poisoning or dismembering tiny bodies, then dumping them in a landfill or garbage disposal."

Those who advocate legal abortion, on the other hand, argue that a fetus is only a potential human being. Therefore, they contend, the rights of the mother—including the right to choose whether she has a baby or not—supersede the rights of the fetus. John M. Swomley, professor of social ethics at the St. Paul School of Theology in Missouri, writes that "because the fetus feels no pain, a function of the brain as yet undeveloped, and the woman acts under her own will and conscience, [abortion is] not violence to a human being. . . . It is not enough to say that abortion is not violent. Abortion is a positive decision and not a lesser evil. It gives women control over their lives, their fertility, their education, their vocations, and their responsibility to their families."

This conflict of opinions over whether or not the fetus is a human life—and thus deserving of the protections afforded to humans—has fueled vociferous and sometimes violent debate about the legality of abortion. However, an increasing number of activists on both sides concede that abortion, as a moral issue, is not entirely clear-cut. Some proponents of abortion rights, for example, condemn late-term abortions—abortions that take place in the third trimester of pregnancy, when the fetus is highly developed. As Catherine Weiss, director of the American Civil Liberties Union's Reproductive Freedom Project, explains, "the fetus grows in moral stature—the importance of recognizing its potential life and protecting its potential increases—as the pregnancy advances." In addition, some pro-life advocates agree that abortion is morally acceptable if a woman's life or health may be endangered by taking a pregnancy to term.

Another important point of agreement between pro-choice and pro-life advocates is so obvious that many have failed to recognize it: Both groups would like to see a society in which fewer abortions are performed. Based on this assumption, a group of pro-life and pro-choice individuals have formed Search for Common Ground, a nonprofit organization that works to promote dialogue between both sides of the abortion conflict. The philosophy behind Common Ground is that the angry rhetoric of the current abortion debate creates a deadlock that prevents people from engaging in rational dialogue. As Frederica Mathewes-Green, a pro-life advocate and member of Common Ground, says, "We say 'It's a baby' and our friends on the pro-choice side say, 'No, it's her right,' and the arguments don't even engage each other. It's an endless, interminable argument that can go on for another 25 years if we don't find a way to break through."

Common Ground advocates a new approach to resolving this perpetual disagreement: Instead of trying to agree upon the ethical status of abortion, members attempt to understand why women choose to have abortions and work to reduce the demand for abortion.

At the same time that groups like Common Ground are working to simplify the abortion debate, however, advances in biotechnology are making it more complex. Two recent scientific developments have raised new ethical questions about abortion. One of these developments is doctors' ability to determine, through amniocentesis or blood tests, whether a fetus in the womb might have a serious birth defect such as Down syndrome. A large proportion of pregnant women who are told that their child is likely to be born with Down syndrome elect to have abortions; according to one statistic provided by the Centers for Disease Control and Prevention, the number of Down syndrome children born to white women in Atlanta decreased by 70 percent during the 1980s as the result of abortions. This fact appalls most pro-life proponents, who believe that aborting disabled fetuses is akin to killing off babies judged to be unworthy of life. Pro-choice activists, in contrast, argue that a woman should never be forced to have a child she doesn't want—especially if that child may require hundreds of thousands of dollars in medical care.

Further advances in the ability to detect inherited traits in the womb intensify this controversy. Experts in genetics predict that it will soon be possible to predict the entire genetic makeup of an unborn child. As David Shenk writes in *Harper's Magazine,*

> Will we know too much? Fetal and embryonic karyotypes may ultimately be as legible as a topographical map: Your son will be born healthy; he will be allergic to cashews; he will reach five foot ten and a half inches; math will not come easily to him; in his later years, he will be at risk for the same type of arteriosclerosis that afflicted his great-grandfather.

Shenk and others contend that such capabilities create a new moral predicament. He writes that "the abortion debate, historically an issue in two dimensions (whether or not individuals should have the right to terminate a pregnancy), suddenly takes on a discomfiting third dimension. Should prospective parents who want a child be allowed to refuse a particular type of child?"

The second development in biotechnology that complicates the issue of abortion is interest in conducting scientific research on stem cells. Stem cells, which are culled from human embryos, can be prompted to grow into a wide variety of tissues, which, some researchers believe, could be transplanted into people suffering from such ailments as Alzheimer's disease, diabetes, and certain heart conditions. Although the medical potential of stem cell research is astounding—William Haseltime, head of Human Genome Sciences, states that "this is the first time we can conceive of human immortality"—anti-abortion groups consider embryo research of any kind to be unethical because it kills living embryos. Furthermore, pro-life advocates worry that the practice of embryo research could destigmatize abortion. Commentator John J. Miller states, "Just imagine an abortion counselor telling a young woman that ending her pregnancy will help scientists improve another person's life." Many scientists, on the other hand, contend that there are no moral problems with stem cell research because an embryo is merely a cluster of cells that cannot experience pain.

In the case of stem cell research, many scientists state that human embryos may eventually not be needed, and that stem cells could potentially be extracted from adult humans. However, the debate over whether—and in what cases—abortion is ethical shows no sign of resolution. In *The Ethics of Abortion: At Issue,* ethicists, scholars, and political commentators offer a variety of perspectives on this challenging issue.

1

Abortion Law in the United States: An Overview

John E. Schwenkler, J.D.

John E. Schwenkler, J.D., is an attorney in New York State. He is the author and editor of the Abortion Law Homepage.

In the landmark case of *Roe v. Wade* in 1973, the U.S. Supreme Court ruled that the Constitution's Fourteenth Amendment established a fundamental right for women to obtain abortions, thereby invalidating all state laws prohibiting abortion within the first six months of pregnancy. However, the Supreme Court cases of *Webster* in 1989 and *Planned Parenthood v. Casey* in 1992 expanded states' rights to regulate abortion. The U.S. Congress has the authority to pass laws providing some restrictions on abortion, but hardly ever uses this power. States, because they can provide rights that are not in the federal Constitution, can pass laws that uphold a women's right to abortion.

American abortion law is a rather complex scene and understanding it requires an adequate grasp of the American court system, the system of federalism, the theory of the separation of powers and especially the doctrine of judicial review.

Abortion law in the United States emanates from two basic governmental sources: (1) the legislatures of the several states and territories and (2) the United States (i.e., the "federal") Supreme Court. The state legislatures, being responsible for the production of most criminal laws, are the traditional source of abortion regulation. Thus, from the decline of common law (judicially created) crimes in the early 19th century, to the intervention of the United States (federal) Supreme Court in the 1970's, state legislatures widely criminalized abortion. In 1973, in the landmark case of *Roe v. Wade*, the United States Supreme Court ruled that the Fourteenth Amendment to the United States Constitution provided a fundamental right for women to obtain abortions. The Supreme Court held that the "right to privacy," established by the Court's precedents in the contraception cases of the 1960's and early 70's, assured the freedom of a person to

Reprinted from John E. Schwenkler, J.D., "Overview," found on the Abortion Law Homepage at http://members.aol.com/_ht_a/abtrbng/overview.htm. Reprinted with permission from the author.

abort unless the state had a "compelling interest" in preventing the abortion. The Court then held that, though the state had an interest in protecting fetal life, this interest did not become "compelling" (i.e., adequate to allow banning an abortion) until fetal viability occurred in the third trimester of pregnancy. Thus, all the state abortion laws that regulated abortion during the first six months of pregnancy (except for the purpose of protecting maternal health during the second trimester) were invalidated.

What this means is that before *Roe v. Wade* in 1973, the legality of abortion essentially rested with the legislatures of the several states. However, in 1973, the Supreme Court made it an issue of federal constitutional law by holding that abortion was a constitutional right. From then on, whether abortion was legal or not depended on the Supreme Court's decisions as to how broad the *Roe* right to abortion actually was. State legislatures continue to have a say only in the little room the Court has left outside the scope of the abortion right.

States' rights to regulate abortion

However, with *Webster* in 1989 and *Planned Parenthood v. Casey* in 1992, the Supreme Court expanded this room, allowing the states that want to regulate abortion substantially more latitude to do so. Since 1992, elective abortions can be banned after actual viability (c. 20–22 weeks), and previability regulations only have to meet the new "undue burden" standard, meaning that a "compelling" state interest is not required so long as the law does not present a "substantial obstacle" to obtaining an abortion.

The main focus of this Supreme Court litigation is the conflict between various states that want to make laws either protecting women or the unborn, and abortion rights advocates who want as little government restraint upon the abortion option as possible. The state will argue that there is no constitutional right to abortion, or if there is a right that it is not violated by the law the state wants to enforce. The abortion rights advocates argue that *Roe v. Wade* rightly protected a fundamental human right and that it must not be eroded by politics.

Before Roe v. Wade *in 1973, the legality of abortion essentially rested with the legislatures of the several states. However, in 1973, the Supreme Court made it an issue of federal constitutional law.*

There are other players, however. The United States Congress can pass at least some abortion regulations—but hardly ever does so. Its legislation is subject to the same constitutional scrutiny as state laws. It must also be remembered that each state has its own state constitution and its set of state constitutional rights. Though these rights cannot operate in derogation of federal constitutional rights, they can provide rights that are not in the federal constitution. Thus, a state supreme court can have its own version of *"Roe v. Wade,"* finding an independent right to abortion in that state's own constitution.

The process since 1973

Supreme Court cases (like *Roe* and *Casey*) generally get started when someone, usually an interested organization (e.g., Planned Parenthood) or someone backed by one, brings a law suit in federal court to enjoin the enforcement of a particular state law, claiming that it violates some provision of the U.S. (federal) Constitution. They sue the state (often through some official, like Dallas District Attorney Henry Wade in *Roe v. Wade* or Pennsylvania Governor Robert Casey on *Planned Parenthood v. Casey*). It begins in a U.S. (federal) District Court in the state in question, where one side wins and the other invariably appeals. The case goes on to the U.S. Circuit Court of Appeals (the intermediate appellate court) for the particular federal circuit the state is in. There a panel of judges will "affirm" or "reverse" the decision of the district court below and the loser will petition the United States Supreme Court to hear the case. If the Court refuses then the decision of the circuit court will stand and will be binding law within that circuit. If the Court agrees (by a vote of four) to take the case then the nine-member Court will decide whether it agrees with how the circuit court ruled or not. Whether the Supreme Court strikes down the law or not, its decision as to what the Constitution says will bind every other court in the country, state or federal.

A state supreme court can have its own version of "Roe v. Wade," finding an independent right to abortion in that state's own constitution.

[N.B. This is not always how it goes—*Roe v. Wade,* for example, came directly up from the district court, which is very unusual. Some cases come out of a state court system after a party lost in that state's supreme court. Also, the federal appellate procedures have changed over the years. Very few cases come to the Supreme Court *via* conventional appeal any more. Most are now brought as petitions for a writ of *certiorari,* which are purely "discretionary," so that the busy Court can take only those few cases they think are important.]

[The United States Supreme Court is the final arbiter of so-called "federal issues," which include interpretation of the U.S. Constitution.]

2

Abortion Is a Moral Choice

Henry Morgentaler

Henry Morgentaler is the founding president of the Humanist Association of Canada and the author of Abortion and Contraception. *He has opened abortion clinics across Canada, often in the face of strong opposition.*

Contrary to what pro-life activists and even some defenders of legal abortion believe, abortion is an extremely moral choice that benefits women and society. Access to legal abortion upholds women's right to control their destinies and allows children to be born into homes where they will be loved and cared for. Most important, abortion reduces the number of unwanted children— some of whom become criminals as a result of parental abuse or neglect. Reproductive choice is clearly an important aspect of a society committed to the ideals of peace, justice, and freedom.

This is a very appropriate time for me to write on "The Moral Case for Abortion." Many people in the pro-choice community believe that the battle for reproductive freedom has been won, that abortion is now available, that women have gained control over their reproductive capacities and have been liberated from the repressive rulings of patriarchal governments. This is not completely true.

There are still many countries in the world where women are subjected to the dogmatic religious edicts of theocracies. There are still women willing to endanger their health, future fertility, and even their lives in order to terminate an unwanted pregnancy. The religious right and the anti-abortion movement is gaining ground on this continent and abroad. Even here, in the United States, where everyone hoped that Roe v. Wade would forever ensure a woman's right to choice, the violent factions of the anti-abortion movement are waging war on doctors, staff, and abortion clinics; and political lobby groups and presidential candidates violently opposed to choice are within reach of the Oval Office. There are even members of the pro-choice community who are questioning the morality of reproductive freedom. These people believe that abortion must be available, but that it is inherently bad—a necessary evil. This

Reprinted from Henry Morgentaler, "The Moral Case for Abortion," *Free Inquiry*, Summer 1996. Reprinted with permission from *Free Inquiry*.

attitude is dangerous and destructive and undermines the enormous gains due to the availability of good abortion services. In fact, the decision to have an abortion is clearly an extremely moral choice; it is a choice that liberates, empowers, and benefits women and society. In this article, I will examine all these issues from a humanist perspective, and reaffirm the morality of reproductive choice.

The issue of the morality of abortion provides the best illustration of the profound difference between humanist ethics and traditional religious attitudes. The former are based on concern for individual and collective well-being and are able to incorporate all available modern data and knowledge; whereas the latter are bound by dogma and tradition to sexist, irrational prohibitions against abortion and women's rights and are completely and callously indifferent to the enormous, avoidable suffering such attitudes are inflicting on individuals and on the community.

Is abortion moral?

Most of the debate raging about abortion around the world has centered around the question of morality. Is it ever moral or responsible for a woman to request and receive an abortion, or is abortion always immoral, sinful, and criminal?

When you listen to the rhetoric of the anti-abortion faction, or read imprecise terms about the unborn, you get the impression that every abortion kills a child; consequently it cannot be condoned under any circumstances, with the sole exception of when the life of the pregnant woman is endangered by the pregnancy, a condition that is now extremely rare. This position—that abortion is always wrong and that there is a human being in the womb from the moment of conception—is a religious idea mostly propagated by the doctrine of the Roman Catholic church and espoused by many fundamentalist Protestant groups, though not by the majority of Catholics and Protestants.

The decision to have an abortion is clearly an extremely moral choice; it is a choice that liberates, empowers, and benefits women and society.

Let us briefly examine this idea. At the moment of conception the sperm and the ovum unite, creating one cell. To proclaim that this one cell is already a full human being and should be treated as such is so patently absurd that it is almost difficult to refute. It is as if someone claimed that one brick is already a house and should be treated with the same respect a full house deserves. Even if you have a hundred bricks, or two hundred bricks, it is not yet a house. For it to be a house it needs walls, plumbing, electricity, and a functional organization. The same is true for a developing embryo. In order for it to be a human being it needs an internal organization, organs, and especially a human brain to be considered fully human. This entity is the result of sexual intercourse, where procreation is often not the goal, and whether it is called a zygote, blastocyst, embryo, or fetus, it does not have all the attributes of a human being and thus cannot properly be considered one.

If abortion is always viewed as "intentional murder," why isn't miscarriage viewed in similar terms? After all, almost half of all embryos are spontaneously shed in what is called "miscarriage" or "spontaneous abortion." If spontaneous abortions are an "act of God," to use the common religious expression, is it not strange that God has so little concern for fetal life that He allows so much of it to go to waste without intervening? Is it not possible to then conclude that God does not mind or object to spontaneous abortions? Why is it that the Catholic church has no ritual to mark the abortion of so much fetal life when it occurs spontaneously, yet becomes so vociferous and condemnatory when it is a conscious decision by a woman or couple?

To proclaim that . . . one cell is already a full human being and should be treated as such is so patently absurd that it is almost difficult to refute.

I believe that an early embryo may be called a potential human being. But remember that every woman has the potential to create twenty-five human beings in her lifetime. The idea that any woman who becomes pregnant as a result of non-procreative sexual intercourse must continue with her pregnancy does not take into consideration the fact that there is a tremendous discrepancy between the enormous potential of human fertility and the real-life ability of women and couples to provide all that is necessary to bring up children properly. The morality of any act cannot be divorced from the foreseeable consequences of that act. Should a girl of twelve or a woman of forty-five, or any woman for that matter, be forced to continue a pregnancy or be saddled with bringing up a child for eighteen years without any regard for the consequences, without any regard for the expressed will or desire of that woman, or of the couple?

Haven't we learned anything by observing events in countries where abortion is illegal, where women are forced to abort fetuses themselves or by the hands of quacks, where many die and more are injured for life or lose their fertility? What about the children often abandoned to institutions where they have no father or mother, where they suffer so much emotional deprivation and trauma that many become psychotic, neurotic, or so full of hate and violence that they become juvenile delinquents and criminals who kill, rape, and maim? When a person is treated badly in his or her childhood, that inner violence manifests itself when he or she is grown up.

The pro-choice philosophy

The pro-choice philosophy maintains that the availability of good medical abortions protects the health and fertility of women and allows children to be born into homes where they can receive love, care, affection, and respect for their unique individuality, so that these children grow up to be joyful, loving, caring, responsible members of the community, able to enter into meaningful relationships with others.

Thus, reproductive freedom—access to legal abortions, to contraception, and, by extension, to sexual education—protects women and couples and is probably the most important aspect of preventive medicine and psychiatry, as well as the most promising preventative of crime and mental illness in our society.

Wherever abortion legislation has been liberalized, particularly in countries where abortion is available upon request, the effects on public health and on the well-being of the community have been very positive. The drastic reduction of illegal, incompetent abortions with their disastrous consequences has almost eliminated one of the major hazards to the lives and health of fertile women. There has been a steady decline in the complications and mortality associated with medical abortions, a decline in mortality due to childbirth, a drop in newborn and infant mortality, an overall decline in premature births, and a drop in the number of births of unwanted children. It is of utmost interest to examine the consequences and effects of the liberalization of the abortion laws.

Where abortion has become legalized and available and where there is sufficient medical manpower to provide quality medical services in this area, the consequences have all been beneficial not only to individuals but also to society in general. In countries where there is a high level of education and where abortions by qualified medical doctors are available without delay, self-induced or illegal abortions by incompetent people

---

The availability of good medical abortions protects the health and fertility of women and allows children to be born into homes where they can receive love, care, affection, and respect.

---

who do not have medical knowledge eventually disappear, with tremendous benefit to the health of women. Also, the mortality connected to medical legal abortions decreases to an amazing degree. In Czechoslovakia in 1978, for instance, the mortality rate was two per 100,000 cases; in the United States it was one death per 200,000 abortions, which is extremely low and compares favorably with the mortality rate for most surgical procedures.

Another medical benefit is that the mortality of women in childbirth also decreases in countries where abortion is legal and the medical manpower exists to provide quality services. This is because the high-risk patients like adolescents, older women, and women with diseases often choose not to continue a high risk pregnancy; consequently, the women who go through childbirth are healthier and better able to withstand the stresses of childbirth; thus, the infant mortality and neonatal mortality has decreased consistently in all countries where abortion has become available.

But probably the biggest benefit of legalized abortion and the one with the greatest impact is that the number of unwanted children is decreasing. Children who are abused, brutalized, or neglected are more likely to become neurotic, psychotic, or criminal elements of society. They become individuals who do not care about themselves or others, who are prone to violence, who are filled with hatred for society and for other people; if the number of such individuals decreases, the welfare of society increases proportionately.

A surprising benefit of abortion

One of the most surprising and beneficial changes going on in both the United States and Canada has been the tremendous decrease in crime, especially violent crime such as murder, rape, and aggravated assault. This trend over the last four years has been proven by impressive statistics collected by the Federal Bureau of Investigators and the police forces of the United States and Canada. The decrease in violent crime is about 8% every year over the last four years. That is quite an impressive trend. Statistics from the province of Quebec, just released April 4, 1996, show a decrease in criminal offenses of 15% every year over the last three years and a decrease of 8% for violent crime. There has been a 30% decrease in crime in New York State, e.g. and many similar statistics in other areas are surprising and extraordinary in view of the prevailing economic uncertainties and disruptions of modern life. What is the explanation?

Some demographers explain this by the fact that there are fewer young men around, and it is mostly young men who commit crimes. No doubt this is true, but what is even more important is that among these young men likely to commit offenses there are fewer who carry an inner rage and vengeance in their hearts from having been abused or cruelly treated as children. Why is that? Because many women who a generation ago were obliged to carry any pregnancy to term now have had the opportunity to choose medical abortion when they were not ready to assume the burden and obligations of motherhood.

Crimes of violence are very often perpetrated by persons who unconsciously want revenge for the wrongs they suffered as children. This need to satisfy an inner urge for vengeance results in violence against children, women, members of minority groups, or anyone who becomes a target of hate by the perpetrator. Children who have been deprived of love and good care, who have been neglected or abused, suffer tremendous emotional harm that may cause mental illness, difficulty in living, and an inner rage that eventually erupts in violence when they become adolescents and adults.

Most of the serial killers were neglected and abused children, deprived of love. Paul Bernardo and Clifford Olson would fit in that category. Both Hitler and Stalin were cruelly beaten by their fathers and carried so much hate in their hearts that when they attained power they caused millions of people to die without remorse. It is accepted wisdom that prevention is better than a cure. To prevent the birth of unwanted children by family planning, birth control, and abortion is preventive medicine, preventive psychiatry, and prevention of violent crime.

I predicted a decline in crime and mental illness twenty-five years ago when I started my campaign to make abortion in Canada legal and safe. It took a long time for this prediction to come true. I expect that conditions will get better as more and more children are born into families that want and deserve them with joy and anticipation.

It is safe to assume that there has been a similar decrease in mental and emotional illness due to the fact that fewer unwanted children are being born. Consequently fewer children suffer the emotional deprivation or abuse that is often associated with being unwanted and undesired. It would be interesting to see appropriate studies to that effect, and I postulate that they would show a dramatic decrease in the overall incidence of mental illness.

Medical abortions on request and good quality care in this area are a tremendous advance not only toward individual health and the dignity of women, but also toward a more loving, caring, and more responsible society, a society where cooperation rather than violence will prevail. Indeed, it may be our only hope to survive as a human species and to preserve intelligent life on this planet in view of the enormous destructive power that mankind has accumulated.

The right to legal abortion is a relatively new achievement, only about twenty-five years old in most countries. It is part of the growing movement of women toward emancipation, toward achieving equal status with men, toward being recognized as full, responsible, equal members of society. We are living in an era where women, especially in the Western world, are being recognized as equal, where the enormous human potential of womankind is finally being acknowledged and accepted as a valuable reservoir of talent. However, women cannot achieve their full potential unless they have freedom to control their bodies, to control their reproductive capacity. Unless they have access to safe abortions to correct the vagaries of biological accidents, they cannot pursue careers, they cannot be equal to men, they cannot avail themselves of the various opportunities theoretically open to all members of our species. The emancipation of women is not possible without reproductive freedom.

> *The biggest benefit of legalized abortion . . . is that the number of unwanted children is decreasing.*

The full acceptance of women might have the enormous consequence of humanizing our species, possibly eliminating war and conflict, and adding a new dimension to the adventure of mankind. Civilization has had many periods of advance and regression, but overall it has seen an almost steady progression toward the recognition of minorities as being human and their acceptance into the overall community. It has happened with people of different nationalities and races. It has happened with prisoners of war, who could be treated mercilessly. It has happened quite recently, actually, with children, who were in many societies considered the property of parents and could be treated with brutality and senseless neglect. It is only a few generations ago that we recognized how important it is for society to treat children with respect, care, love, and affection, so that they become caring, loving, affectionate, responsible adults.

Recognizing the rights of women

Finally, many countries now recognize the rights of women to belong fully to the human species, and have given them freedom from reproductive bondage and allowed them to control their fertility and their own bodies. This is a revolutionary advance of great potential significance to the human species. We are in the middle of this revolution, and it is not surprising that many elements of our society are recalcitrant and are obstructing this progress. They act out of blind obedience to dogma, tradition, and past conditions and are hankering for the times when women were oppressed and considered only useful for procreation, housework, and the care of children.

The real problems in the world—starvation, misery, poverty, and the potential for global violence and destruction—call for concerted action on the part of governments, institutions, and society at large to effectively control overpopulation. It is imperative to control human fertility and to only have children who can be well taken care of, receiving not only food, shelter, and education, but also the emotional sustenance that comes from a loving home and parents who can provide love, affection, and care.

In order to achieve this, women across the world have to be granted the rights and dignity they deserve as full members of the human community. This would naturally include the right to safe medical abortions on request in an atmosphere of acceptance of specifically female needs and in the spirit of the full equality of women and men in a more human and humane society.

Somebody has said that it is impossible to stop the success of an idea whose time has come. But good ideas come and go. Occasionally they are submerged for long periods of time due to ignorance, tradition, resistance to change, and the vested interests of those frightened by change. Occasionally, new and good ideas will gain slow and grudging acceptance. More often, they will be accepted only after a period of struggle and sacrifice by those who are convinced of the justice of their cause. The struggle for reproductive freedom, including the right to safe, medical abortion, could be classified as one of those great ideas whose time has come.

Enormous progress has been made in many countries, including the United States and Canada. But in many other countries, legal abortion is still not available. With the beneficial effects of women's access to abortion and reproductive freedom so obvious to so many people, why is there still so much violent opposition to it? I believe it is due to the fact that people who are bound to traditional religious attitudes resent the newly acquired freedom of women and want to turn the clock back.

Taboos and practices regarding human reproduction and sexuality were written into religious teachings hundreds of years ago, which were then written into the laws of the country. Laws on abortion were introduced long before science enlightened us with the facts concerning embryological development. For instance, in the Catholic church it was thought that, at the moment of conception, a fully formed person, termed a homunculus, lived in the mother's womb, and had only to develop to a certain size to be expelled from it. That belief was held in the distant past, but the effect of the imagery still remains, resulting in the Catholic belief that abortion is the murder of a live human being.

Historically, and even up to this day, men hold the authority in all the major religions of the world. In most countries men are also heads of state and lawmakers. In science and medicine, men traditionally hold the reins of authority and power, only recently allowing women entry into these fields. Is it any wonder then, that laws and attitudes regarding abortion took so long to change? But now these attitudes are changing, and women around the world are gradually acquiring more power and more control of their reproductive capacities. Unfortunately, organized religions, propelled by traditional dogma and fundamentalist rhetoric, are fueling the fires of the anti-choice movement with lying, inflammatory propaganda and violent rhetoric leading to riots and murder. The anti-choice supporters realize they have lost the battle, that public opinion has not been swayed by their diatribes and dogmatic opposition. Consequently, they are angry and increasingly engaging in terrorist tactics. Their recourse to violence, both in the United States and Canada, resulting in the murder and wounding of doctors performing abortions and the increasing violence directed at abortion providers, is a sign of moral bankruptcy, but unfortunately it places the lives of all physicians and medical staff who provide abortions in danger.

For those who believe that the so-called pro-life have occupied the high moral ground in the debate on abortion, I say, "Rubbish." They have never been on a high moral ground, they only pretend to occupy this elevated position by cloaking their oppressive beliefs under the lofty rhetoric of "the defense of innocent unborn life" or "the struggle against the death dealing abortion industry" and similar misleading and blatantly false propaganda. As well, the recourse by the anti-choice movement to violence and murder in order to impose their so-called morality on the whole of society certainly robs them of any credibility. In view of this, it is hard for me to understand the defeatist attitude of some people in the pro-choice community in the United States and their attempt to justify abortion as a necessary evil for which we should all apologize.

When a feminist with impressive credentials and many books to her credit such as Naomi Wolf talks of abortion as a "sin or frivolous," starts feeling guilty about it, and wants everyone who is engaged in providing abortions to repent for their sins, there is something definitely wrong. Were she alone I could believe it is a personal idiosyncrasy. However, there are others in the pro-choice community who attempt to justify themselves and their actions with an attitude that says, "Yes, we need abortions to help some women, but we deplore the fact that we have to do them, our hearts are not really in it, and it would be nice if we did not have to do it."

What is going on here? Have all these people forgotten that women used to die in our countries from self-induced or quack abortions, that unwanted children were given away to institutions where they suffered enormous trauma that took the joy of life away from them and made them into anxious, depressed, individuals with a grudge against society? Have all these people forgotten that an unwanted pregnancy was the biggest health hazard to young fertile women and could result in loss of fertility, long-term illness, injury, and death?

Let us keep in mind the positive accomplishments of reproductive freedom that I mentioned earlier. An abortion need not be a traumatic event; it often is a liberating experience for the woman, who is able to make an important decision in her life, who exercises her right to choose what is best for her. That is the meaning of freedom, of empowerment.

A choice that is empowering and liberating

A woman's choice to terminate a pregnancy is both empowering and liberating. It empowers her because her choice acknowledges that she understands her options, her current situation, and her future expectations, and she is able to make a fully informed decision about what would most benefit her and act on it. It liberates her because she can regain control of her reproductive system and chart her destiny without an unwanted child in tow. It liberates her to fully care for her existing family, her career, her emotional and mental well-being, and her goals.

It is our job as abortion providers to respect the choices of women and to provide abortion services with competence, compassion, and empathy. I wish to suggest that under such conditions women do not necessarily view their abortion as negative, but, on the contrary, and in spite of regrets at having to make such a choice, see it as a positive and enriching experience where their choices are respected and they are treated with the dignity they deserve in such a difficult situation.

> *An abortion need not be a traumatic event; it often is a liberating experience for the woman, who is able to make an important decision in her life.*

Doctors and clinic workers have been in a stressful situation for many years, subject to threats, insults, and moral condemnation. Over the last four years the threats have escalated from verbal abuse to murder. Yet most of us have not given up. Most of us continue to provide excellent abortion services to women in spite of all the threats because we are committed to protection of women's health and to the liberation of women, to the empowerment of women and couples and to a better society with freedom for all. I wish to salute all those health professionals who, in spite of intimidation and threats of death, are continuing every day to treat women with competence, empathy, and compassion.

I wish to conclude on a personal note. Over the years many people have asked me: "Why did you decide to expose yourself to so much stress and danger in a controversial cause, and why do you persist in doing so?" The answer, after a great deal of reflecting upon it, is the following:

I am a survivor of the Nazi Holocaust, that orgy of cruelty and inhumanity of man to man. As such, I have personally experienced suffering, oppression, and justice inflicted by men beholden to an inhuman, dogmatic, irrational ideology. To relieve suffering, to diminish oppression and injustice, is very important to me. Reproductive freedom and good access to medical abortion means that women can give life to wanted babies at a time when they can provide love, care, and nurturing. Well-loved children grow into adults who do not build concentration camps, do not rape, and do not murder. They are likely to enjoy life, to love and care for each other and the larger society.

By fighting for reproductive freedom, I am contributing to a more caring and loving society based on the ideals of peace, justice, and freedom, and devoted to the full realization of human potential. Having known myself the depth of human depravity and cruelty, I wish to do whatever I can to replace hate with love, cruelty with kindness, and irrationality with reason.

This is why I am so passionately dedicated to the cause I defend and why I will continue to promote it as long as I have a valid contribution to offer.

3

Abortion Is Not a Moral Choice

John Paul II

John Paul II is the pope of the Roman Catholic Church.

Abortion cannot be justified under any circumstance because it constitutes the killing of an innocent human being at the very beginning of life. Pro-choice activists attempt to defend abortion by claiming that an unborn baby cannot be considered a person. However, modern science has clearly confirmed that human life begins at the moment of fertilization. Furthermore, the mere probability that a human embryo constitutes a human life warrants the complete prohibition of abortion. Abortion should be recognized for what it is: the murder of a sacred human life.

"*Your eyes beheld my unformed substance*" (Ps. 139:16): the unspeakable crime of abortion.

Among all the crimes which can be committed against life, procured abortion has characteristics making it particularly serious and deplorable. The Second Vatican Council defines abortion, together with infanticide, as an "unspeakable crime."

But today in many people's consciences the perception of its gravity has become progressively obscured. The acceptance of abortion in the popular mind, in behavior and even in law itself, is a telling sign of an extremely dangerous crisis of the moral sense, which is becoming more and more incapable of distinguishing between good and evil even when the fundamental right to life is at stake. Given such a grave situation, we need now more than ever to have the courage to look the truth in the eye and to call things by their proper name, without yielding to convenient compromises or to the temptation of self-deception. In this regard the reproach of the prophet is extremely straightforward: "Woe to those who call evil good and good evil, who put darkness for light and light for darkness" (Is. 5:20). Especially in the case of abortion there is a widespread use of ambiguous terminology, such as *interruption of pregnancy*, which tends

Excerpted from Pope John Paul II, "Evangelium Vitae," *Origins*, April 6, 1995.

to hide abortion's true nature and to attenuate its seriousness in public opinion. Perhaps this linguistic phenomenon is itself a symptom of an uneasiness of conscience. But no word has the power to change the reality of things: Procured abortion is the deliberate and direct killing, by whatever means it is carried out, of a human being in the initial phase of his or her existence, extending from conception to birth.

Abortion is murder

The moral gravity of procured abortion is apparent in all its truth if we recognize that we are dealing with murder and, in particular, when we consider the specific elements involved. The one eliminated is a human being at the very beginning of life. No one more absolutely innocent could be imagined. In no way could this human being ever be considered an aggressor, much less an unjust aggressor! He or she is weak, defenseless, even to the point of lacking that minimal form of defense consisting in the poignant power of a newborn baby's cries and tears. The unborn child is totally entrusted to the protection and care of the woman carrying him or her in the womb. And yet sometimes it is precisely the mother herself who makes the decision and asks for the child to be eliminated, and who then goes about having it done.

> *Abortion is the deliberate and direct killing . . . of a human being in the initial phase of his or her existence.*

It is true that the decision to have an abortion is often tragic and painful for the mother insofar as the decision to rid herself of the fruit of conception is not made for purely selfish reasons or out of convenience, but out of a desire to protect certain important values such as her own health or a decent standard of living for the other members of the family. Sometimes it is feared that the child to be born would live in such conditions that it would be better if the birth did not take place. Nevertheless, these reasons and others like them, however serious and tragic, can never justify the deliberate killing of an innocent human being.

Who bears responsibility

As well as the mother, there are often other people too who decide upon the death of the child in the womb. In the first place, the father of the child may be to blame, not only when he directly pressures the woman to have an abortion, but also when he indirectly encourages such a decision on her part by leaving her alone to face the problems of pregnancy: In this way the family is thus mortally wounded and profaned in its nature as a community of love and in its vocation to be the "sanctuary of life." Nor can one overlook the pressures which sometimes come from the wider family circle and from friends. Sometimes the woman is subjected to such strong pressure that she feels psychologically forced to have an abortion: Certainly in this case moral responsibility lies particularly with those who have directly or indirectly obliged her to have an abortion. Doctors and nurses are also responsible when they place at the service of death skills which were acquired for promoting life.

But responsibility likewise falls on the legislators who have promoted and approved abortion laws and, to the extent that they have a say in the matter, on the administrators of the health care centers where abortions are performed. A general and no less serious responsibility lies with those who have encouraged the spread of an attitude of sexual permissiveness and a lack of esteem for motherhood, and with those who should have ensured—but did not—effective family and social policies in support of families, especially larger families and those with particular financial and educational needs. Finally, one cannot overlook the network of complicity which reaches out to include international institutions, foundations and associations which systematically campaign for the legalization and spread of abortion in the world. In this sense abortion goes beyond the responsibility of individuals and beyond the harm done to them, and takes on a distinctly social dimension. It is a most serious wound inflicted on society and its culture by the very people who ought to be society's promoters and defenders. As I wrote in my letter to families, "We are facing an immense threat to life: not only to the life of individuals but also to that of civilization itself." We are facing what can be called a "structure of sin" which opposes human life not yet born.

The embryo is a human life

Some people try to justify abortion by claiming that the result of conception, at least up to a certain number of days, cannot yet be considered a personal human life. But in fact, "from the time that the ovum is fertilized, a life is begun which is neither that of the father nor the mother; it is rather the life of a new human being with his own growth. It would never be made human if it were not human already. This has always been clear, and . . . modern genetic science offers clear confirmation. It has demonstrated that from the first instant there is established the program of what this living being will be: a person, this individual person with his characteristic aspects already well determined. Right from fertilization the adventure of a human life begins, and each of its capacities requires time—a rather lengthy time to find its place and to be in a position to act." Even if the presence of a spiritual soul cannot be ascertained by empirical data, the results themselves of scientific research on the human embryo provide "a valuable indication for discerning by the use of reason a personal presence at the moment of the first appearance of a human life: How could a human individual not be a human person?"

Furthermore, what is at stake is so important that, from the standpoint of moral obligation, the mere probability that a human person is involved would suffice to justify an absolutely clear prohibition of any intervention aimed at killing a human embryo. Precisely for this reason, over and above all scientific debates and those philosophical affirmations to which the magisterium has not expressly committed itself, the church has always taught and continues to teach that the result of human procreation, from the first moment of its existence, must be guaranteed that unconditional respect which is morally due to the human being in his or her totality and unity as body and spirit: "The human being is to be respected and treated as a person from the moment of conception, and therefore from that same moment his rights as a person must be recognized, among which in the first place is the inviolable right of every innocent human being to life."

The texts of Sacred Scripture never address the question of deliberate abortion and so do not directly and specifically condemn it. But they show such great respect for the human being in the mother's womb that they require as a logical consequence that God's commandment "you shall not kill" be extended to the unborn child as well.

Human life is sacred and inviolable at every moment of existence, including the initial phase which precedes birth. All human beings, from their mothers' womb, belong to God who searches them and knows them, who forms them and knits them together with his own hands, who gazes on them when they are tiny shapeless embryos and already sees in them the adults of tomorrow whose days are numbered and whose vocation is even now written in the "book of life" (cf. Ps. 139:1, 13–16). There too, when they are still in their mothers' womb—as many passages of the Bible bear witness—they are the personal objects of God's loving and fatherly providence.

Human life is sacred and inviolable at every moment of existence.

Christian tradition—as the declaration issued by the Congregation for the Doctrine of the Faith points out so well—is clear and unanimous from the beginning up to our own day in describing abortion as a particularly grave moral disorder. From its first contacts with the Greco-Roman world, where abortion and infanticide were widely practiced, the first Christian community, by its teaching and practice radically opposed the customs rampant in that society, as is clearly shown by the Didache mentioned earlier. Among the Greek ecclesiastical writers, Athenagoras records that Christians consider as murderesses women who have recourse to abortifacient medicines, because children, even if they are still in their mother's womb, "are already under the protection of divine providence." Among the Latin authors, Tertullian affirms: "It is anticipated murder to prevent someone from being born; it makes little difference whether one kills a soul already born or puts it to death at birth. He who will one day be a man is a man already."

Throughout Christianity's 2,000-year history, this same doctrine has been constantly taught by the fathers of the church and by her pastors and doctors. Even scientific and philosophical discussions about the precise moment of the infusion of the spiritual soul have never given rise to any hesitation about the moral condemnation of abortion.

The Church's condemnation of abortion

The more recent papal magisterium has vigorously reaffirmed this common doctrine. Pius XI in particular, in his encyclical *Casti Connubii,* rejected the specious justifications of abortion. Pius XII excluded all direct abortion, i.e., every act tending directly to destroy human life in the womb "whether such destruction is intended as an end or only as a means to an end." John XXIII reaffirmed that human life is sacred because "from its very beginning it directly involves God's creative activity." The Second Vatican Council, as mentioned earlier, sternly condemned abortion: "From the moment of its conception life must be guarded with the greatest care, while abortion and infanticide are unspeakable crimes."

Direct abortion . . . always constitutes a grave moral disorder.

The church's canonical discipline from the earliest centuries has inflicted penal sanctions on those guilty of abortion. This practice, with more or less severe penalties, has been confirmed in various periods of history. The 1917 Code of Canon Law punished abortion with excommunication. The revised canonical legislation continues this tradition when it decrees that "a person who actually procures an abortion incurs automatic (*latae sententiae*) excommunication." The excommunication affects all those who commit this crime with knowledge of the penalty attached and thus includes those accomplices without whose help the crime would not have been committed. By this reiterated sanction, the church makes clear that abortion is a most serious and dangerous crime, thereby encouraging those who commit it to seek without delay the path of conversion. In the church the purpose of the penalty of excommunication is to make an individual fully aware of the gravity of a certain sin and then to foster genuine conversion and repentance.

Given such unanimity in the doctrinal and disciplinary tradition of the church, Paul VI was able to declare that this tradition is unchanged and unchangeable. Therefore, by the authority which Christ conferred upon Peter and his successors, in communion with the bishops—who on various occasions have condemned abortion and who in the aforementioned consultation, albeit dispersed throughout the world, have shown unanimous agreement concerning this doctrine—*I declare that direct abortion, that is, abortion willed as an end or as a means, always constitutes a grave moral disorder,* since it is the deliberate killing of an innocent human being. This doctrine is based upon the natural law and upon the written word of God, is transmitted by the church's tradition and taught by the ordinary and universal magisterium.

No circumstance, no purpose, no law whatsoever can ever make licit an act which is intrinsically illicit, since it is contrary to the law of God which is written in every human heart, knowable by reason itself and proclaimed by the church.

4

The Morality of Abortion Is Difficult to Determine

Ted Merrill

Ted Merrill practices emergency medicine in Portland, Oregon, and is a board-certified family practitioner.

Extreme views about the morality of abortion—whether these views are pro-life or pro-choice—fail to represent the complexity of the issue and do not hold up under close examination. For example, a group of pro-choice students found that after studying live chick embryos, their feelings about abortion were no longer entirely clear-cut. The question of abortion requires society to make subtle and difficult judgments about right and wrong.

Strange as it may seem, I routinely murmur "excuse me" before I swat a fly. I can't butcher a chicken without apologizing first. I have grieved for the cat that died beneath the wheels of my car.

Yes, I hold all life sacred. But I'm also a pragmatist. I believe that the necessity of making choices forces us to view the sacredness of life as relative. That's why I performed a small number of abortions when I was in family practice. I never did them without exploring all available options—for both the patient and myself. I also referred a few patients elsewhere for abortions I couldn't do in good conscience.

Yet I am not pro-abortion. Nor am I against it. Anyone who is convinced of the absolute rightness of either position doesn't fully understand the situation. Any argument that doesn't express a certain amount of ambivalence rings hollow to me.

Extreme positions do not hold up

Extreme positions may be easier when the argument is intellectual. But they don't hold up at close range. I noticed this in my interactions with college students in an anatomy and physiology class I taught. The nine students in this all-female class were unequivocally in favor of abortion

Reprinted from Ted Merrill, "Abortion: Extreme Views Ignore Reality," *Medical Economics*, July 15, 1996. Reprinted with permission from *Medical Economics*.

rights when we started the section on reproduction. But something changed when they studied live chick embryos.

I had explained to them that all vertebrates closely resemble one another during early development. Then we opened fertilized eggs at various stages. Under a microscope, eggs that have incubated for 36 hours show the first rudiments of an embryo, and a crude tubular structure rhythmically twitching in the center. At 48 hours, you can see an elementary—but definitely formed—heart pumping real blood cells through a looped network of tubes. You can recognize an eye. Just a day later, there are limbs, a face, and a brain that looks like linked sausages.

As the young women looked at these early-stage embryos and watched that amazing little heart beating, they were moved. "If we closed up the shell and put it back in the incubator, would it still grow?" one of them asked me. Another said, "It's going to die in a little while under the microscope, isn't it?" A third student declared, "I don't think we should be doing this." And while some of my students couldn't wait to see how the embryo progressed through the later stages of development, others became upset and refused to open any more eggs.

When I brought the talk around to abortion again, I noticed that their feelings were no longer clear-cut. They all upheld a woman's right to choose, but felt that other factors had to be considered, too.

Anyone who is convinced of the absolute rightness of either position [on abortion] doesn't fully understand the situation.

I suspect the same dynamic was involved when Norma McCorvey—the "Jane Roe" of the 1973 Roe vs. Wade Supreme Court decision—had a change of heart while working in an abortion clinic. McCorvey never did have the abortion, but she became an abortion-rights activist years after the court decision. Then a confluence of events made her realize that she could never have an abortion herself, even while she supported free choice in principle. Newspaper accounts say the turning point was witnessing a second-trimester abortion and seeing a clinic worker put the fetus into a freezer. Whatever the reason, deeper immersion into the reality of abortion added a new dimension to McCorvey's thinking.

A dimension that is difficult to see

The one dimension that's difficult to see, of course, is how the lives of many people would be changed if abortions weren't done. The patients for whom I performed abortions, most of them married women whose birth control had failed, had that to consider. None of them made the decision lightly.

Like any worthwhile question, abortion requires us to seek reality and truth. It forces us to wrestle with conflicting values and find a workable solution for each particular situation. When faced with such a difficult choice, all we can do is take our very best shot at making the right decision.

5

Abortion Is Sometimes Necessary

Naomi Wolf

Naomi Wolf, an adviser to President Bill Clinton on feminist issues, is the author of The Beauty Myth: How Images of Beauty Are Used Against Women, Fire with Fire: The New Female Power and How to Use It, *and* Promiscuities: The Secret Struggle for Womanhood.

Those who support legal abortion must reconsider the pro-choice notion that abortion is simply "a woman's choice." Instead, pro-choice activists must acknowledge that abortion is a grave moral decision, but one that is sometimes necessary. Improved access to contraception is one step society can take to reduce the likelihood of abortion.

From a pro-choice point of view, things look grim. In March 1997 came accusations that abortion-rights advocates had prevaricated about how frequently "partial birth" or "intact dilation and evacuation" abortion is performed. Then the House of Representatives voted overwhelmingly to ban the procedure. The Senate may soon address the issue, but even if it fails to override President Clinton's promised veto, the pro-choice movement is staring at a great symbolic defeat. [President Clinton vetoed the measure.]

This looks like a dark hour for those of us who are pro-choice. But, with a radical shift in language and philosophy, we can turn this moment into a victory for all Americans.

How? First, let us stop shying away from the facts. Pro-lifers have made the most of the "partial birth" abortion debate to dramatize the gruesome details of late-term abortions. Then they moved on to the equally unpleasant details of second-trimester abortions. Thus, pro-lifers have succeeded in making queasy many voters who once thought that they were comfortable with Roe v. Wade.

Unfortunately, we set ourselves up for this. Our rhetoric has long relied on euphemism. An abortion was simply "a woman's choice." We clung to a neutral, abstract language of "privacy" and "rights." This ap-

Reprinted from Naomi Wolf, "Pro-Choice and Pro-Life," *The New York Times*, April 3, 1997. Reprinted with permission from *The New York Times*.

proach was bound to cede the moral high ground to our opposition and to guarantee an erosion of support for abortion rights. Thirty percent of Americans support abortion based on the "woman's choice" argument alone, but when people are asked whether abortion should be a matter between "a woman, her doctor, her conscience and her God," 70 percent agree.

Hunger for a moral framework

By ignoring this hunger for a moral framework around legal abortion, we inadvertently played into the drama that was performed before Congress. When someone holds up a model of a six-month-old fetus and a pair of surgical scissors, we say, "choice," and we lose.

Some pro-choicers have recently resorted to heartless medicalese to explain away the upsetting details of late abortions, pointing out that no major surgery is pretty. Such responses make us seem disconnected from our own humane sensibilities. We should acknowledge what most Americans want us to: that abortion at any stage, since it involves the possibility of another life, is a grave decision qualitatively different from medical choices that involve no one but ourselves.

What if we transformed our language to reflect the spiritual perceptions of most Americans? What if we called abortion what many believe it to be: a failure, whether that failure is of technology, social support, education, or male and female responsibility? What if we called policies that sustain, tolerate and even guarantee the highest abortion rate of any industrialized nation what they should be called: crimes against women?

Acknowledging abortion as a necessary evil

If we frankly acknowledged abortion as a necessary evil, a more effective and ethical strategy falls into place. Instead of avoiding pictures of mangled fetuses as if they were pro-life propaganda, we could claim them as our own most eloquent testimony.

Rolling back abortion rights would merely ease lawmakers' consciences, while many women, and more late-term fetuses than are aborted now, would die in back alleys, deaths as agonizing as those that pro-lifers have been so graphically describing. No woman, we should argue, should have to make the terrible choice of a late abortion if there is any alternative. And these late abortions are more likely to occur when 80 percent of women have to travel outside of their counties to end a pregnancy.

Abortion at any stage, since it involves the possibility of another life, is a grave decision.

The moral of such awful scenes is that a full-fledged campaign for cheap and easily accessible contraception is the best antidote to our shamefully high abortion rate. Use of birth control lowers the likelihood of abortion by 85 percent, according to the Alan Guttmacher Institute.

More than half of unplanned pregnancies occur because no contraception was used. If we asked Americans to send checks to Planned Parenthood to help save hundreds of thousands of women a year from having to face abortions, our support would rise exponentially.

Use of birth control lowers the likelihood of abortion by 85 percent.

A year of sexual responsibility can easily cost someone $200 or more (and that someone is likely to be female). To those who oppose access to contraceptives, yet hold up images of dead fetuses, we should say: This disaster might have been prevented by a few cents' worth of nonoxynol-9; this blood is on your hands.

For whatever the millions of pro-lifers think about birth control, abortion must surely be worse. A challenge to pro-choicers to abandon a dogmatic approach must be met with a challenge to pro-lifers to separate from the demagogues in their ranks and join us in a drive to prevent unwanted pregnancy.

Bringing together activists from both sides

The Common Ground Network for Life and Choice has brought activists together from both sides. They are working on insuring better prenatal care; making adoption easier; reducing the rate of teen pregnancy through programs that give girls better opportunities and offer them mentors; and rejecting violent means of protest. They have teamed abortion clinics to prenatal care and adoption clinics to give desperate women real choices. The network has even found that half of the pro-lifers in some of its groups would support a campaign to improve access to birth control.

The pro-choice movement should give God a seat at the table. For many good reasons, including the religious right's often punitive use of Scripture and the ardently anti-abortion position of the Roman Catholic Church, the pro-choice movement has been wary of God-based arguments.

But on issues of values like abortion and assisted suicide, the old Marxist-Freudian, secular-materialist left has run out of both ideas and authority. The emerging "religious left" is where we must turn for new and better ideas. We should call on the ministers, priests and rabbis of the religious left to explain their support of abortion rights in light of what they understand to be God's will.

Unspoken religious assumptions play a part

America is a religious country—and a pluralistic one. Even in debate about "partial birth" abortion, unspoken religious assumptions and differences play a part. While Judaism generally maintains that in a choice between the fetus and the mother, the mother's life, with its adult obligations, must always come first, traditional Catholic teaching holds that you cannot directly kill a fetus to save the life of the mother. Americans must be reminded that people of faith can reach different conclusions about abortion.

Finally, we must press Congress to work with the Clinton Administration to take this approach at the national level. On Jan. 22, 1997, Hillary Rodham Clinton, Vice President Al Gore and Tipper Gore took the extraordinary step of calling on abortion providers and their opponents to reject extremism, support efforts to lower the abortion rate and talk with those who do not share their views.

Now lawmakers must follow through with sweeping policies to give that sentiment substance. Congress and the Administration should champion the "common ground" approach, and add to it bipartisan support for financing far more research, development and distribution of contraceptives.

We have all lived with the human cost of our hypocrisies for too long. It is time to abandon symbolic debates on Capitol Hill in favor of policies that can give women—who have been so ill-served by the rigid views on both sides—real help and real choice.

6

The Myth of Abortion as a "Necessary Evil"

Clarke D. Forsythe

Clarke D. Forsythe is the attorney and president of Americans United for Life in Chicago.

Most Americans regard legal abortion as an evil that is "necessary" to prevent dangerous back-alley abortions that kill or injure women. This belief is based solely on myth. In reality, back-alley abortions were never common, nor are legal abortions entirely safe. The assertion that abortion is a "necessary evil" is a means by which the pro-choice movement soothes society's moral qualms about a procedure that is clearly wrong.

Twenty-six years after the Supreme Court's Roe v. Wade decision, the public debate on abortion seems to have reached a stalemate. The issue continues to be debated in Congress and state legislatures across the country, but, year to year, there seems to be little change in public opinion.

This does not mean, however, that the abortion issue is going to recede in intensity any time soon. There are many reasons for this, but perhaps the most important is simply that "the majority of Americans morally disapprove of the majority of abortions currently performed," as University of Virginia sociologist James Hunter concludes in his pathbreaking 1994 book, *Before the Shooting Begins: Searching for Democracy in America's Culture Wars*. Hunter's analysis is based on the 1991 Gallup poll "Abortion and Moral Beliefs," the most thorough survey of American attitudes toward abortion yet conducted.

The Gallup study found that 77 percent of Americans believe that abortion is at least the "taking of human life" (28 percent), if not "murder" itself (49 percent). Other polls confirm these findings. And yet, while many Americans—perhaps 60 percent in the middle—see legalized abortion as an evil, they see it as "necessary."

The *Chicago Tribune* aptly summarized the situation in a September 1996 editorial: "Most Americans are uncomfortable with all-or-nothing policies on abortion. They generally shy away from proposals to ban it in virtually all circumstances, but neither are they inclined to make it avail-

Reprinted from Clarke D. Forsythe, "Abortion Is Not a 'Necessary Evil,'" *Christianity Today*, May 24, 1999. Reprinted with permission from the author.

able on demand no matter what the circumstances. They regard it, at best, as a necessary evil."

If Middle America—as Hunter calls the 60 percent—sees abortion as an evil, why is it thought to be necessary? Although the 1991 Gallup poll did not probe this question specifically, it made clear that it is not because Middle America sees abortion as necessary to secure equal opportunities for women. For example, less than 30 percent believe abortion is acceptable in the first three months of pregnancy if the pregnancy would require a teenager to drop out of school (and the number drops below 20 percent if the abortion is beyond three months). Likewise, less than 20 percent support abortion in the first three months of pregnancy if the pregnancy would interrupt a woman's career (and that support drops to 10 percent if the abortion is after the third month).

Four "necessary" myths

Instead, many Americans, therefore, may see abortion as "necessary" to avert "the back alley." In this sense, the notion of legal abortion as a "necessary evil" is based on a series of myths widely disseminated since the 1960s. These myths captured the public mind and have yet to be rebutted.

The notion of legal abortion as a "necessary evil" is based on a series of myths widely disseminated since the 1960s.

Myth #1: One to two million illegal abortions occurred annually before legalization. In fact, the annual total in the few years before abortion on demand was no more than tens of thousands and most likely fewer. For example, in California, the most populous state where it was alleged that 100,000 illegal abortions occurred annually in the 1960s, only 5,000 abortions were performed in 1968, the first full year of legalization.

Myth #2: Thousands of women died annually from abortions before legalization. As a leader in the legalization movement, Dr. Bernard Nathanson later wrote: "How many deaths were we talking about when abortion was illegal? In N.A.R.A.L. we generally emphasized the drama of the individual case, not the mass statistics, but when we spoke of the latter it was always '5,000 to 10,000 deaths a year.' I confess that I knew the figures were totally false, and I suppose that others did too if they stopped to think of it. But in the 'morality' of our revolution, it was a useful figure, widely accepted, so why go out of our way to correct it with honest statistics?"

In fact, the U.S. Centers for Disease Control (CDC) statistics in 1972 show that 39 women died from illegal abortion and 27 died from legal abortion.

Myth #3: Abortion law targeted women rather than abortionists before legalization. In fact, the nearly uniform policy of the states for nearly a century before 1973 was to treat the woman as the second victim of abortion.

Myth #4: Legalized abortion has been good for women. In fact, women still die from legal abortion, and the general impact on health has had many negative consequences, including the physical and psychological toll that many women bear, the epidemic of sexually transmitted disease, the general coarsening of male-female relationships over the past 30 years, the threefold increase in the repeat-abortion rate, and the increase in hospitalizations from ectopic pregnancies.

Seeing little alternative to legalized abortion

A generation of Americans educated by these myths sees little alternative to legalized abortion. It is commonly believed that prohibitions on abortion would not reduce abortion and only push thousands of women into "the back alley" where many would be killed or injured. Prohibitions would mean no fewer abortions and more women injured or killed. Wouldn't that be worse than the status quo?

Middle America's sense that abortion is a necessary evil explains a lot of things, and, by giving coherent explanation to many disparate facts and impressions, it may provide a way beyond the stalemate to—as Hunter calls for—an elevation in the content and conduct of the public debate.

First, this notion of abortion as a necessary evil explains the seemingly contradictory polls showing that a majority of Americans believe both that abortion is murder and that it should be legal. The most committed pro-life Americans see legality and morality to be inextricably intertwined and therefore view the polling data as contradictory. But Middle America understands "legal" versus "illegal" not in moral terms but in practical terms—criminalizing the procedure. Based on the historical myths, Middle America believes that criminalizing abortion would only aggravate a bad situation.

Second, the myth of abortion as a necessary evil also explains the power of the "choice" rhetoric. For the most committed abortion proponents, "choice" means moral autonomy. But there are less ideological meanings. According to the choice rhetoric, Americans can persuade women to make another choice, but they can't make abortion illegal, because that would mean no fewer abortions and simply push women into the back alley. This explains why Middle America will support virtually any regulation, short of making abortions illegal, that will encourage alternatives and reduce abortions. In a sense, by supporting legal regulations but not prohibitions, many Americans may believe that they are choosing "the lesser of two evils."

A key tactic of abortion advocates

The rhetoric of abortion as a "necessary evil" (though not the phrase itself) is a key tactic of abortion advocates. It is roughly reflected in President Clinton's slogan that he wants abortion to be "safe, legal, and rare" and is at the heart of the President's veto of the federal partial-birth abortion bill. In the face of polls showing that 70 to 80 percent of Americans oppose the procedure, the President says that the procedure is horrible (it's an evil) but contends that "a few hundred women" every year must have the procedure (it's necessary).

Indeed, the rhetoric of abortion as a necessary evil is designed to sideline Americans' moral qualms about abortion. For example, when Congress first began to consider the bill prohibiting partial-birth abortion, abortion advocates bought a full-page advertisement in the New York Times showing a large coat hanger and the caption, "Will this be the only approved method of abortion?" The coat hanger, reinforcing the image of the back alley, remains a powerful rhetorical symbol. It reinforces the notion that there are two and only two alternatives: abortion on demand or the back alley.

The coat hanger . . . remains a powerful rhetorical symbol. It reinforces the notion that there are two and only two alternatives: abortion on demand or the back alley.

Finally, the myth of abortion as a "necessary evil" also explains why 49 percent of Americans may believe that abortion is "murder" without translating this into fervent social or political mobilization. While Middle Americans may view abortion as an evil, they view it as intractable. For this reason, they view fervent campaigns to prohibit abortion as unrealistic if not counterproductive, while they are drawn to realistic alternatives and regulations. They agree that there are too many abortions and would like to see them reduced. Abortion is not a galvanizing electoral issue for Middle America, because Middle America doesn't see that much can be done about the issue legally or politically.

The future of abortion

The myth of abortion as a necessary evil has serious implications for future public debate. First, it means that abortion opponents have won the essential debate that the unborn is a human being and not mere tissue. In fact, the whole thrust of the "choice" argument admits this and seeks to sideline Americans' moral qualms by telling Americans that, even if it is a human life, the most that can be done is to persuade women not to have abortions.

Second, it means that the ideological arguments of both sides ("choice" versus "child") often miss the much more practical concerns of many Americans.

Third, it means that Americans balance the fate of the woman and the fate of the child. Although they understand the fate of the child to be fatal, they want to avoid the same result for women and believe that legalized abortion has been good generally for women.

This means that maximizing the fatal impact of abortion through, for example, graphic pictures of aborted babies is not a "silver bullet" that will transform public opinion alone. Instead, elevating the content and conduct of the public debate requires addressing both aspects—the impact on women as well as the impact on the child. Helping the public understand the impact on both, and the alternatives available, may contribute to a renewal of public dialogue that we so sorely need on this issue.

But a renewal of the public dialogue won't mean much if the people are not allowed to express the public will on this issue, as they usually do in our democratic republic. Twenty-six years ago, the Supreme Court claimed hegemony over the issue and created a nationwide rule of abortion on demand, preventing democratic debate and solutions. The public policy dictated by the Supreme Court collides with majority opinion and reflects the views of only the 20 percent who are committed to abortion on demand. Twenty-six years later, that is the main reason the pot keeps boiling.

7

Legal Abortion
Is a Social Right

Marlene Gerber Fried

Marlene Gerber Fried is an activist with the Reproductive Rights Network and the National Network of Abortion Funds. She is also the director of the Civil Liberties and Public Policy Program at Hampshire College.

Before abortion was made legal, thousands of women died each year from complications associated with back-alley abortions. *Roe v. Wade* protected women's right to a safe, legal abortion; however, that right is currently threatened by abortion opponents, whose violent methods of protest have created a climate in which women fear to have abortions and doctors fear to provide them. Unobstructed access to abortion is an important aspect of any human rights, feminist, and social justice agenda.

The 25th anniversary of *Roe v. Wade* produced a media barrage of articles, television, movies, talk shows and opinion polls showing that a majority of Americans believe abortion should be legal but restricted. These polls tell us that most people in the United States do not share the view that abortion should be available when needed, for any woman, for any reason. In 1998 this is apparently as radical a position as it was in 1973.

At the same time, millions of women continue to have abortions at close to the rate they have had them for many years. Abortion remains the most common surgical procedure in the country. This means that many of those who say abortion is murder have had or will have them.

The recent polls also show that a majority of people in the U.S. believe that the anti-abortion movement is extremist. At the same time, those polled give high marks to anti-abortion activists for being "principled." It seems that the anti-abortion movement is perceived as resorting to its violent measure, such as the recent clinic bombing in Alabama, because of an ethical position. Conversely, while pro-choice activists are viewed as more "reasonable" and "moderate," we are often not viewed as holding an ethical position.

Reprinted from Marlene Gerber Fried, "Legal But . . . Framing the Ethics of Abortion Rights," *RESIST Newsletter*, April 1998. Reprinted with permission from Resist, Inc., 259 Elm St., Somerville, MA 02114, www.resistinc.org.

How should we understand this complicated picture of abortion today? And how, after so many years of battle, do we assess what pro-choice activists have accomplished? What inroads have the anti-abortion movement made when, although abortion has not significantly declined, high levels of violence against clinics and their personnel are tolerated? How we answer these questions will direct the fight for reproductive freedom in the future.

Abortion-rights activists face a two-fold challenge. The first piece of it is long-term and ideological, as well as legal: to find the language, strategies and allies to guarantee every woman a fundamental right to make her own reproductive choice. Secondly, and simultaneously, we have to interrupt a widespread complacency and engage a sense of urgency about the reproductive rights agenda.

One way of both challenging the ethics of the anti-abortion movement and highlighting the urgent, unmet needs is to resurrect for ourselves and for public discussion the history of abortion.

"The deaths stopped overnight"

There is overwhelming documentation from the criminal era, beginning in the mid 1800s, of death and serious health consequences from illegal abortion. Before *Roe* 1,000 to 5,000 women died annually from abortion-related complications. In the 1920s and 1930s abortion accounted for 14% of all maternal deaths, with higher rates in urban areas. Race and class were significant factors—the death rate for women of color was four times that for white women.

The safety of abortion was a political matter. The same methods which reduced mortality in childbirth and in surgery in general—the introduction of antiseptics in the late 1800s and sulfa drugs and penicillin in the 1930s—were the means to make abortion safe. While these methods were used for the relatively small number of therapeutic abortions (legal procedures which became increasingly restricted), abortion mostly remained dangerous because it was criminalized.

Before Roe *1,000 to 5,000 women died annually from abortion-related complications.*

Roe transformed abortion from a life-threatening and terrifying experience to a safe one for those women who had access to it. With the passage of *Roe* the mortality rates dropped dramatically. A coroner who worked at a hospital in Pennsylvania before legalization said it simply, "The deaths stopped overnight in 1973, and I never saw another abortion death in all the eighteen years after that until I retired. That ought to tell people something about keeping abortion legal." (*The Worst of Times*, Patricia G. Miller, Harper, 1993, p. 13) Today a first trimester abortion in the U.S. done in appropriate settings is as safe as a tonsillectomy.

Twenty-one million women have had thirty-five million abortions since *Roe v. Wade*. The pre-*Roe* figures are more difficult to come by, but what we do know tells us that abortion was quite common then as well.

In the first half of the 1800s, before criminalization, an estimated 25% of all pregnancies were aborted. In the 1920s and 1930s there were an estimated 1.2 to 2 million abortions a year—or roughly 20% of all pregnancies in the 1920s. Kinsey's study in the 1950s found that white upper and middle class women aborted 24.3% of their pregnancies; 64% of unmarried white women had abortions and 40% of unmarried black women. (*When Abortion Was a Crime,* Leslie J. Reagon, University of California Press, 1997)

Our own history, and contemporary data from countries where abortion continues to be illegal or severely restricted, underscores the pervasiveness of abortion regardless of its legal status. It reminds us that the legal status of abortion does not affect whether women have them. It does determine the toll on the lives and health of women. Although we have not yet done so, successfully publicizing this history could be the basis of clarifying the public health and moral aspects of abortion.

Reframing the issues

The reality of abortion has been framed by its opponents, and the picture is a distorted one. The anti-abortion movement pretends that widespread abortion was caused by legalization and denies the consequences of criminalization. Perhaps most problematic and pervasive is the characterization that women themselves fall into two categories: those who want to have babies and the others who want abortions. The truth is that the same women are having babies and abortions, just at different times in their lives.

The extent of the success of abortion opponents in framing the issue is evident in the polls about the morality of abortion. Fifty percent of respondents say they think abortion is murder. At the same time, almost one-third of those also think that abortion is sometimes the best course of action. So while respondents seem to understand the need for legal abortion, they have trouble claiming it as a moral choice. The implication is that it is acceptable to have an abortion just so long as you understand that you are doing the wrong thing. This position ensures that stigma, silence and guilt will continue to surround abortion. For example, a 1997 graduate of Yale Medical School reported that the word "abortion" was never mentioned throughout her four years there. As one reporter put it, "In America, abortion is discussed, abortions are not." (*U.S. News & World Report,* January 19, 1998, p. 20)

In focus group research, young pro-choice women are more sympathetic to abortion if the woman had responsible sex, but not if she failed to use contraception. What do we make of this? Why is motherhood deemed appropriate "punishment" for failure to practice effective birth control? It seems that the "personal responsibility" campaigns of the right—in the welfare reform, as well as teen pregnancy debates—have been successful in shaping these opinions. This suggests the importance of engaging the realities of contraception—their failures; the conditions of women's lives, including abuse, that make it difficult to use birth control consistently; a culture that still refuses to talk candidly about sexual activity: a campaign to teach abstinence-only curricula.

The larger issue, however, is that the pro-choice movement must decide to confront the widespread moral ambivalence about abortion rather than hoping to evade it with the notion of choice. Given the fact that women continue to have abortions at sustained rates, we have, too often, deemed such views irrelevant. The "murder but" position is fertile ground for opponents of abortion to exploit, as we have seen in their efforts to ban D & X (so called "partial birth") abortions.

The anti-abortion movement understands the politics of morality. It has been able to turn ethical qualms into restrictive policies which mostly burden women without power and resources. We have feared that engaging in moral discussion cedes too much ground. But refusing to do so has left morality to the opposition. The right to abortion does rest on ethical principles which require that morality be grounded in the reality of women's lives, which make women's autonomy central, and which prioritize access issues because they are questions of social justice.

Anti-abortion violence as "ethics"

Any discussion of the ethics of abortion cannot ignore anti-abortion violence. The recent murder of a security guard and serious injury to a nurse at an abortion clinic in Alabama vividly illustrates an ongoing strategy of terrorizing not only the clinic staff who are the direct targets, but women seeking abortions and the general public. The focus group research cited earlier showed that young women felt it would be dangerous to become activists for reproductive freedom. Certainly the anti-abortion movement has created a climate in which promoting or providing abortion services means risking one's life.

Since the early 1980s anti-abortion violence aimed at clinics has been escalating. Although it appeared to have peaked in 1994 with the murders at abortion clinics in Florida and Massachusetts, it continues. The 1997 Clinic Violence Survey Report (conducted by the Feminist Majority Foundation, released January 15, 1998) illustrates the current pattern of anti-abortion violence. Severe violence still plagues 25% of clinics. There were 13 women's health clinic bombings or arsons in 1997. At the same time the percentage of clinics not experiencing violence, harassment, or intimidation has doubled over the last four years. Anti-abortion violence is becoming ever more concentrated on a small number of clinics which are subjected to multiple types of violence on a daily basis. In addition to other kinds of attacks, activists against abortion routinely threaten clinic workers and sometimes stalk their children, harm their pets, and damage their property.

Activists against abortion routinely threaten clinic workers and sometimes stalk their children, harm their pets, and damage their property.

The chilling effect of such deeds is felt at every clinic in the country as evidenced by the attrition of clinic staff, clinic closings, stepped up levels of security, increased stress. For abortion providers an "ordinary" day includes doctors wearing bullet proof vests, women coming for abortions passing through metal detectors, and sweeps for bombs. Forty-five states have fewer providers than ten years ago; the number of hospitals providing abortions decreased by 600 between 1978 and 1988 and another 18% between 1988 and 1992. The report analyzes this as a "war of attrition" in which one set of clinics and health care workers are targeted, the violence causes workers to quit and perhaps the clinic to close, and then the anti-choice forces move on to another clinic. In 1993, one in five clinics had staff members resign because of clinic violence.

Even relatively few incidents of deadly violence inspire pervasive terror and create an overall climate of fear and intimidation. This is part of its purpose. The bomb used in Alabama was built to inflict maximum damage to people, not to property. Last year in Atlanta the double bombing of a clinic marked the first time anti-abortionists had used an anti-personnel bomb targeted at rescue and law enforcement personnel. Thus far all of the murders have been abortion clinic workers—two doctors, one escort, two receptionists, a security guard, a nurse/counselor. But who dies is only a tactical question for the anti-abortion movement.

Obstructing women's rights

After the Brookline, Massachusetts murders there were appeals by pro-choice advocates to the anti-abortion movement to tone down its language. But these calls—by those who saw a clear link between rhetoric and action—have not been heeded. "Execute abortionists" signs were in evidence in Washington, DC, at the anti-*Roe v. Wade* demonstration. The "Nuremberg Files" web site lists the names, addresses and social security numbers of 300 doctors, clinic workers, law enforcement personnel, politicians and judges. Inflammatory rhetoric is not confined to the so-called anti-choice "extremists." The mainstream of that movement says it opposes anti-abortion violence, but it also fuels it by insisting that such violence is caused by the violence of abortion.

Anti-abortion violence is simply not treated with the same degree of intolerance as other forms of violence. As has been observed before, if hundreds of banks rather than abortion clinics were being targeted we would see a very different response. "Innocent officer killed" was the *Boston Globe* headline after the Alabama bombing. The paper was only echoing the statements of a law enforcement spokesman who wanted to be sure to note that the security guard was not involved in the abortion issue. In Florida a doctor complained to the local sheriff about threats to himself and to his clinic. The sheriff responded that he would do everything he could to support the demonstrators.

The issue here is not whether the sheriff is entitled to his own beliefs. The question is whether it is permissible for him to refuse to uphold the law. Surely the answer must be no.

Abortion is the only medical procedure which has a "conscience clause." This exemption allowing doctors not to learn about or to perform abortions has already given permission for an increasing range of people to claim moral legitimacy for obstructing women's decisions. A pharmacist in California refused to fill a prescription for emergency contraception. Over 80% of pharmacists surveyed thought they had the right to refuse to fill prescriptions for drugs like RU 486 in accordance with their moral beliefs. An anti-choice doctor in Massachusetts refused to write her patient a prescription for birth control pills. A receptionist at a local hospital told women, falsely, that the hospital did not provide abortion services. An insurance company worker refused to provide a woman with a referral for an abortion.

As with anti-abortion violence, pro-choice advocates should neither see nor respond to these as if they were isolated cases. The anti-abortion movement encourages its members to obstruct wherever they can, and the societal response has been one of tolerance. We must challenge that tolerance.

Why should OB GYNs be permitted to refuse to perform the most common surgical procedure that women undergo? I am not suggesting that they be forced to do abortions. I am suggesting that they not be OB GYNs if they cannot offer women the full range of basic care. Similarly, medical schools should not be permitted to refuse to teach abortion when (if the current trend persists) 43% of women will have had at least one in their lifetime. And hospitals cannot permit anti-abortion nurses to treat abortion patients with hostility. They must be held accountable and either refuse to allow nurses who won't participate to work in OB GYN, or be sure that an adequate number of nurses are available who will be involved in abortions.

Our ethical concerns in these cases should not rest with making sure that an individual's rights to act in accordance with one's own beliefs is protected. We must also be concerned that institutional policies protect women's rights by ensuring access to abortion and create a climate in which women having abortions are treated with care and respect. The marginalization of abortion within mainstream medicine and the stigmatizing of both those who perform abortions and those who have them will have to be fought.

Expanding abortion access

Throughout its existence, Reproductive Rights Network has framed the fight for abortion rights in the larger context of reproductive freedom for all women. But we did not foresee how hard we would have to fight just to hold on to past gains. *Roe* was supposed to be the first step toward expanding reproductive and sexual freedom for women. Instead it has become a glass ceiling which the anti-abortion movement continues to try to lower. While keeping the big picture in mind, we continue to work against the erosion of abortion access which cause terrible hardships for the most vulnerable women—young women, low-income women of whom a disproportionate number are women of color, and rural women.

Thousands of women must overcome incredible obstacles to get their abortions, and thousands more cannot obtain them. Conservative estimates tell us that one in five Medicaid-eligible women are in this situation. Abortion services have been virtually eliminated in large parts of the country, and there is a critical shortage of abortion providers and services.

Fighting for access is especially difficult in this period of privatization and victim blaming. Punitive welfare reform strategies that limit the possibilities for poor women to have children are just the other side of the abortion restriction coin, and we must build alliances with welfare rights advocates. Ultimately, securing abortion access requires that abortion services become part of comprehensive health care available to all women, and part of an even larger human rights, feminist and social justice agenda. Despite the fact that we are very far from this, even as an ideal, we must take it as a goal. Concretizing this sweeping prescription into workable strategies and an ethical perspective is perhaps our most acute challenge.

8

Legal Abortion
Is a Social Injustice

First Things

First Things *is a monthly journal that discusses issues of religion and public life.*

The Supreme Court's ruling on *Roe v. Wade* in 1973 has created a society that endorses the large-scale killing of unborn children. The majority of the American public never supported—and still do not accept—"liberalized" abortion laws; therefore, the radical pro-abortion regime created by *Roe* is a violation of the democratic principle of self-government. Moreover, abortion is a monumental act of social and moral injustice that is comparable to slavery.

Twenty-five years ago, on January 22, 1973, the Supreme Court of the United States, in what numerous constitutional scholars have called an act of raw judicial power, abolished the abortion laws of all fifty states. The news went out that the Court had settled the controversy over abortion. A generation later there is no more unsettled and unsettling question in American public life, and a settlement is nowhere in sight. For the next generation as well, it seems possible that abortion will be the bloody crossroads where conflicting visions of the kind of people we are and should be will do battle.

In an editorial following the *Planned Parenthood v. Casey* decision of 1992, we wrote:

> For years, some of us have been writing about the "culture wars" in which our society is embroiled. We are two nations: one concentrated on rights and laws, the other on rights and wrongs; one radically individualistic and dedicated to the actualized self, the other communal and invoking the common good; one viewing law as the instrument of the will to power and license, the other affirming an objective moral order reflected in a Constitution to which we are obliged; one given to private satisfaction, the other to familial responsibility; one typically secular, the

Reprinted from *First Things*, "Roe: Twenty-Five Years Later," January 1998. Reprinted with permission from *First Things*.

other typically religious; one elitist, the other populist. The strokes are admittedly broad, but the reality is evident enough to anyone who attends to the increasingly ugly rancor that dominates and debases our public life. And, of course, for many Americans the conflicts in the culture wars run through their own hearts.

What the abortion debate is about

One might argue whether the two nations are more or less divided today, but the reality has not substantively changed. No other question cuts so close to the heart of the culture wars as the question of abortion. The abortion debate is about more than abortion. It is about the nature of human life and community. It is about whether rights are the product of human decision or, as the Founders declared, an endowment from our Creator. In the words of Pope John Paul II in the encyclical *Evangelium Vitae,* the abortion debate is about the conflict between "the culture of life and the culture of death." It is about euthanasia, eugenic engineering, and the protection of the radically handicapped. Press almost any of the great social and moral disputes in our public life and, usually sooner rather than later, the argument turns to abortion. That is what it means to say that abortion is the bloody crossroads.

Abortion will be the bloody crossroads where conflicting visions of the kind of people we are and should be will do battle.

In *Roe v. Wade* and related decisions, the Supreme Court has gambled its authority, and with it our constitutional order, by coming down on one side of this great conflict. The result is a clear declaration of belligerency on one side of the culture wars. And one result of that is a constitutional crisis created by what is aptly described as the judicial usurpation of politics. Another result weighs even more heavily on those who believe—in accord with all scientific evidence and sound reasoning—that the life terminated by abortion is a human being. Not in a distant time and place, but in our time and in our land we have witnessed these past twenty-five years the legal killing of approximately thirty-five million innocent unborn children. We do well to recoil when it is put so bluntly. The desperate search for euphemism is understandable, but it is in vain.

Remember how it happened. The conventional telling of the story is that the Court only gave a nudge to what was already happening. The author of the majority opinion, the late Justice Harry Blackmun, opined, "Roe against Wade was not such a revolutionary opinion at the time." Justice Ruth Bader Ginsburg has said that the radical decision of *Roe* was unnecessary because society was already moving toward the same result of its own accord. The conventional telling of the story is false. When the *Roe* decision came down, pro-abortionists and anti-abortionists alike expressed amazement at the sweeping change that the Court had imposed upon the country. A "liberalization" of existing law was expected by most; the abolition of all law protecting the unborn was expected by almost nobody outside the Court itself.

The radical abortion regime

It is twenty-five years later and most Americans still do not believe how radical is the abortion regime imposed by *Roe.* The pro-abortion media persist in reporting that the law permits abortion in the early months of pregnancy and only for compelling reasons, and many prefer to think that is so. In fact, abortion is legal at any time for any reason during the entire pregnancy, and, as partial-birth abortion makes starkly clear, beyond. In the regime of *Roe* and its judicial progeny, psychological distress triggers a constitutional right to abortion, even if the distress is occasioned by being denied an abortion. The new order imposed by the Court is abortion on demand. Some object to that phrase. Call it abortion on request or free market abortion. Whatever it is called, it is the unlimited right to the private use of lethal force against innocent human beings.

Not in a distant time and place, but in our time and in our land we have witnessed . . . the legal killing of approximately thirty-five million innocent unborn children.

We may seek moral shelter behind claims that it is not *really* a human being, that it is only a potential human being, that it does not look like a human being. But we know that nothing that is not a human being has the potential of becoming a human being, and nothing that has the potential of becoming a human being is not a human being. We hold against it that it is totally dependent, but it will be as dependent one month outside the womb as it is one month inside the womb. Nor can we entirely repress the knowledge that, in the moral tradition that formed our culture, the condition of dependence obliges others to be dependable. As for it not looking like a human being, the embryo or fetus, or call it what we will, is exactly what a human being looks like at that age. It is what each of us looked like when we were that old.

We must never lose sight of the fact that the abortion regime of *Roe* was arrogantly imposed by the Court. At the time, the country was *not* moving toward liberalized abortion, never mind abortion on demand. This is amply documented also in pro-abortion writings such as David Garrow's history, *Liberty and Sexuality: The Right to Privacy and the Making of Roe v. Wade.* It began with contraception when in *Griswold v. Connecticut* (1965) the Court "invented" (Garrow's word) the right to privacy, the putative right on which *Roe* was later based. Until then, the opponents of restrictions on contraceptive devices had failed to win a single legislative victory. As for abortion, Alan Guttmacher of Planned Parenthood flatly said in 1963 that any abortion law suggesting the non-humanity of the fetus would "be voted down by the body politic." He was right. It is true that in 1970 New York and Hawaii "liberalized" their abortion laws, but the changes were narrow and contentious, and it is generally acknowledged that in New York opinion was shifting back to support for laws protective of the unborn.

[Legal abortion] is the unlimited right to the private use of lethal force against innocent human beings.

The larger picture was unmistakably clear. In 1967, "reform" measures, usually limited to therapeutic exceptions, were turned back in Arizona, Georgia, New York, Indiana, North Dakota, New Mexico, Nebraska, and New Jersey. In 1969, such bills failed to get out of committee in Iowa and Minnesota, and were defeated outright in Nevada and Illinois. In 1970, exceptions based on therapeutic reasons were defeated in Vermont and Massachusetts. In 1971, on the eve of *Roe,* repeal bills were voted down in Montana, New Mexico, Iowa, Minnesota, Maryland, Colorado, Massachusetts, Georgia, Connecticut, Illinois, Maine, Ohio, and North Dakota. In 1972, at the very time the Court was considering *Roe,* the Massachusetts House by a landslide vote of 178 to 46 passed a measure that would have bestowed the full legal rights of children on fetuses, from the moment of conception. At the same time, the supreme courts of South Dakota and Missouri upheld state anti-abortion laws. At the moment Justice Harry Blackmun was putting the finishing touches on his opinion in *Roe,* 61 percent of the voters in Michigan and 77 percent in North Dakota voted down repeal. Everywhere, in every test, the voters overwhelmingly rejected the doctrine that individuals are answerable to no one other than themselves in the matter of abortion. In the face of that reality, the Court imposed the regime of *Roe.* That is what is meant by an act of raw judicial power.

The message of *Casey*

In 1997, writing for a tenuously unanimous Court, Chief Justice William Rehnquist refused to invent a constitutional right to assisted suicide, noting the political dangers of abolishing the existing laws of virtually all the states. Although the 1973 decision was not mentioned explicitly, there was no mistaking the reference to *Roe.* The Court acknowledged that it dare not do again what it did in *Roe.* Yet *Roe* was left untouched. While a majority of the Court is not prepared to say that *Roe* was rightly decided and some Justices say it was a monumental error, it is a decision that the Court is afraid to correct. That is the indisputable message of *Casey,* in which the astonishing assertion is made that the legitimacy of the Court and the rule of law itself depends upon the American people accepting the abortion regime imposed by *Roe.*

The proper response to that claim was offered by a broad array of Christian leaders in the statement "We Hold These Truths":

> In *Casey* the Court admonished pro-life dissenters, chastising them for continuing the debate and suggesting that the very legitimacy of the law depends upon the American people obeying the Court's decisions, even though no evidence

is offered that those decisions are supported by the Constitution or accepted by a moral consensus of the citizenry. If the Court is inviting us to end the debate over abortion, we, as Christians and free citizens of this republic, respectfully decline the invitation.

That statement also declares:

Our goal is unequivocal: Every unborn child protected in law and welcomed in life. We have no illusions that, in a world wounded by sin, that goal will ever be achieved perfectly. . . . [But] we are convinced that the Court was wrong, both morally and legally, to withdraw from a large part of the human community the constitutional guarantee of equal protection and due process of law.

The American people as a whole have not accepted, and we believe they will not accept, the abortion regime imposed by *Roe v. Wade.* In its procedural violation of democratic self-government and in its substantive violation of the "laws of nature and of nature's God," this decision of the Court forfeits any claim to the obedience of conscientious citizens. We are resolved to work relentlessly, through peaceful and constitutional means and for however long it takes, to effectively reverse the abortion license imposed by *Roe v. Wade.* We ask all Americans to join us in that resolve.

That is, we believe, precisely the right response and the necessary resolve. As many others have done, the religious leaders point to the ominous parallels with the infamous *Dred Scott* decision about slavery in 1857. At the time of that decision, there seemed to be little hope for its reversal, and it was reversed in fact only by the bloodletting of civil warfare. God willing, we do not face the prospect of another civil war. It is impossible to imagine what civil war would mean today. But the cleavage in our society over abortion and related questions touching on respect for human life is deep and ominous, comparable only to the cleavage over slavery. In the way that we now look back on slavery, we hope that Americans of the next century will look back with deepest shame on the abortion regime of *Roe.*

In the way that we now look back on slavery, we hope that Americans of the next century will look back with deepest shame on the abortion regime of Roe.

Twenty-five years is a long time in our political history, a short time in the human story. Many Americans refuse to recognize the horror of abortion on demand, many have gotten used to it, and a substantial number support it. *Casey* was right in saying that the American people are being tested by the regime of *Roe,* but the test is whether we have the decency and the will to overthrow it. Elections are important to that testing. It seems quite possible that the next President will appoint four Justices to the Supreme Court. Also important are fresh legislative initiatives at the state and federal levels, persistent activism, and unrelenting public education. And prayer without ceasing.

The culture of death commands a formidable array of powerful institutions. With few exceptions, it has in its service the establishment media, the universities, the foundations, the corporate elites, the labor unions, the oldline churches, and, of course, the courts. More than any other question in public dispute, abortion on demand is the core commitment of the American establishment. The institutional base of the culture of life seems pitiably weak by comparison. But on the side of the goal of "every unborn child protected in law and welcomed in life" is moral truth, and what we must hope is the enduring, if sometimes inarticulate, decency of most Americans. This people, we must also hope, have not entirely lost their taste for self-government. They have not agreed to be ruled by nine unelected lawyers on the Supreme Court. They have not, in the words of Lincoln's First Inaugural Address, "practically resigned their government into the hands of that eminent tribunal."

Roe v. Wade will, one way or another, sooner or later, be a nightmare past. Millions of lives depend upon it, our moral self-respect depends upon it, our constitutional order depends upon it, the rule of law depends upon it. Join prayer to resolve that the way be peaceful and the end be sooner rather than later.

9

Finding Common Ground in the Abortion Debate

Frederica Mathewes-Green

Frederica Mathewes-Green is the author of Real Choices: Listening to Women Looking for Alternatives to Abortion.

The antagonistic rhetoric of the abortion debate creates animosity between pro-life and pro-choice groups and fails to acknowledge that the two groups share a common goal: to create a society in which women no longer want abortions. The pro-life movement's message that abortion kills an unborn child alienates women who support abortion rights; similarly, the pro-choice assertion that anti-abortion advocates are "against choice" or "sexist" estranges pro-lifers. Common Ground, an organization that promotes discussion between pro-life and pro-choice activists, attempts to reframe the abortion debate by searching for beliefs shared by both sides. Among the organization's goals are to establish a database of agreed-upon facts about abortion, find ways to prevent unwanted pregnancies, promote adoption as an alternative to abortion, and help women who become pregnant unintentionally to cope.

At one point in my life I was prochoice, but I came over to a prolife position years ago. I've been there ever since. Perhaps because of my background, I think there's a logic to the prochoice position that deserves respect, even as we engage it critically. It is possible to disagree with people without calling them baby-killers, without believing that they are monsters or fiends. It is possible to disagree in an agreeable way. The abortion argument is essentially an argument among women. It's been a bitter and ugly debate, and I find that embarrassing.

What the two sides have in common is this: Each of us would like to see a world where women no longer want abortions.

I don't believe that even among the most fervent prochoice people there is anybody who rejoices over abortion. I think we both wish that there were better solutions that could make abortion unnecessary, or

Reprinted from Frederica Mathewes-Green, "We Can Find Common Ground on Abortion," *U.S. Catholic*, January 1998. Reprinted with permission from the author.

prevent pregnancies in the first place. We'd like to see the demand for the procedure reduced, by resolving women's problems and alleviating the pressure for abortion. We can go along this road together as far as we can, and there will come a time when prochoicers are satisfied and prolifers want to keep going, but that doesn't mean we can't go together for now.

A few years ago, quite by accident, I discovered an important piece of common ground. Something I wrote in a conservative think-tank journal was picked up and quoted widely. I had written: "There is a tremendous sadness and loneliness in the cry 'A woman's right to choose.' No one wants an abortion as she wants an ice-cream cone or a Porsche. She wants an abortion as an animal, caught in a trap, wants to gnaw off its own leg."

What the two sides [of the abortion debate] have in common is this: each of us would like to see a world where women no longer want abortions.

What surprised me was where it appeared: I started getting clips in the mail from friends, showing the quote featured in prochoice publications. I realized I had stumbled across one of those points of agreement: we all know that no one leaves the abortion clinic skipping. This made me think that there was common ground, that instead of marching against each other, maybe we could envision a world without abortion, a world we could reach by marching together.

Behind enemy lines

The problem thus far—and I believe the prolife movement has been especially complicit in this—is that we have focused only on abortion and not on women's needs. We in the prolife movement have perpetuated a dichotomy where it's the baby against the woman, and we're on the baby's side. You can look over 25 years of prolife rhetoric and basically boil it down to three words: "It's a baby." We have our little-feet lapel pins, our "Abortion stops a beating heart" bumper stickers, and we've pounded on that message.

In the process we have contributed to what I think is a false concept—an unnatural and even bizarre concept—that women and their unborn children are mortal enemies. We have contributed to the idea that they've got to duke it out, it's going to be a fight to the finish. Either the woman is going to lose control of her life, or the child is going to lose its life.

It occurred to me that there's something wrong with this picture. Nature puts mother and child together; it doesn't make them enemies; it doesn't set one against the other in a battle to the death.

If our rhetoric is tearing them apart, we're the ones who are out of step. When we presume this degree of conflict between women and their own children, we're locating the conflict in the wrong place.

The problem is not located inside women's bodies, it's within society. Social expectations make unwanted pregnancy more likely to occur and harder for women to bear. Unwed mothers are supposed to have abortions, to save the rest of us from all the costs of bringing an "unwanted" child into the world.

There are three drawbacks to emphasizing "It's a baby" as the sole message. One is that it contributes to the present deadlock in this debate. We say, "It's a baby," and our friends on the prochoice side say, "No, it's her right," and the arguments don't even engage each other. It's an endless, interminable argument that can go on for another 25 years if we don't find a way to break through.

Second, the "It's a baby" message alienates the woman distressed by a difficult pregnancy. There's a prolife message I sometimes hear that makes me cringe: "Women only want abortions for convenience. They do this for frivolous reasons. She wants to fit into her prom dress. She wants to go on a cruise." This alienates the very person to whom we need to show compassion. If we're going to begin finding ways to live without abortion, we need to understand her problems better.

No one leaves the abortion clinic skipping.

Of course, there has been a wing of the prolife movement that has been addressing itself to pregnant women's needs for a long time, and that is the crisis-pregnancy-center movement. Centers like these have been giving women maternity clothes, shelter, medical care, job training, and other help for 30 years. I once saw a breakdown of the money and time spent on various sorts of prolife activities, and over half the movement's energy was going into direct aid to pregnant women. Yet you don't hear this in the rhetoric.

The third problem with this rhetoric is that it enables the people in the great mushy middle, the ones who are neither strongly prolife nor strongly prochoice, to go on shrugging off the problem. While both sides know that women don't actually want abortions in any positive sense, the middle is convinced they do.

Prolifers say, "She wants an abortion because she's selfish"; prochoicers say, "She wants an abortion because it will set her free." No wonder the middle believes us: it's one of the few things we appear to agree on.

Both sides know that abortion is usually a very unhappy choice. If women are lining up by the thousands every day to do something they do not want to do, it's not really liberation that women have won. And yet the middle thinks that abortion is what women want, so there's no need for change and nothing to fix.

I can understand why my prolife allies put the emphasis on "It's a baby." It's a powerful and essential message. Visualizing the violence against the unborn was the conversion point for me and many others. But it cannot be our sole message.

Polls on U.S. attitudes toward abortion show that between 70 and 80 percent already agree that it's a baby—especially since the advent of sonograms. So when we say, "It's a baby," we're answering a question nobody's asking anymore. The real question is, "How could we live without abortion?"

Preventing unwanted pregnancies

The abortion rate in this country is about 1.5 million a year, a rate that has held fairly stable for about 15 years. Divide that figure by 365 and that equals about 4,000 abortions every day. It's a sobering figure.

The shortsighted prolife response has been, "Put a padlock on the abortion store." But that's not going to solve the problem. You cannot reduce the demand by shutting off the supply. If 4,000 women were lining up every day to get breast implants, we'd ask, "What's causing this demand? What's going on here?"

Solving the problems that contribute to the demand for abortion will not be easy. The two obvious components are: preventing unwanted pregnancies in the first place, and assisting women who slip through the cracks and become pregnant anyway.

The obvious tool for pregnancy prevention is contraception, but the prolife movement has been reluctant to support the contraceptive option. Being an Orthodox Christian, I come from a religious tradition that permits some forms of contraception, so it's not been a theological problem for me.

So when I started considering this, I thought, "This is great! I'll get a helicopter, fill it with condoms, get a snow shovel, and just fly over the country tossing 'em out. We'll close all of the abortion clinics tomorrow!"

But then I began to analyze a little deeper. While I believe the prolife movement needs to make a strong stand in favor of preventing these unplanned pregnancies, I became skeptical of the contraceptive solution.

For example, there's the recent study showing that about two thirds of births to teenage moms in California involved a dad who was an adult. Another study found that teen mothers had been forced into sex at a young age and that the men who molested them had an average age of 27.

Social expectations make unwanted pregnancy more likely to occur and harder for women to bear.

Closer to home, a friend of mine was brought to an abortion clinic by her older brother, who molested her when she was 12; they gave her a bag of condoms and told her to be more careful. You're not going to solve problems like these by tossing a handful of condoms at them.

But leaving aside the question of sexual abuse, I think we need to look hard at the consequences of the sexual revolution that began in the 1960s. When I entered college in the early 1970s, the revolution was in full bloom. It seemed, at the time, a pretty carefree enterprise. Condoms, pills, and diaphragms were readily available, and abortion had just been legalized by the U.S. Supreme Court.

But I gradually began to think that it was a con game being played on women. We were "expected to behave according to men's notions of sexuality," to use author Adrienne Rich's phrase. Instead of gaining respect and security in our bodies, we were expected to be more physically available, more vulnerable than before, with little offered in return.

What women found out is that we have hearts in there along with all our other physical equipment, and you can't put a condom on your heart.

So in answering the question "How do we live without abortion?", I'd say we need to look at restoring respect and righting the balance of power in male-female sexual relationships.

The mom stands alone

What can we do to help women who get pregnant and would rather not be? For my book *Real Choices,* I went around the country talking to women who have had an abortion and to women who provide care for pregnant women. I had presumed that most abortions are prompted by problems that are financial or practical in nature.

But to my surprise, I found something very different. What I heard most frequently in my interviews was that the reason for the abortion was not financial or practical. The core reason I heard was, "I had the abortion because someone I love told me to." It was either the father of the child, or else the woman's own mother, who was pressuring her to have the abortion.

Again and again, I learned that women had abortions because they felt abandoned—they felt isolated and afraid. As one woman said, "I felt like everyone would support me if I had the abortion; but if I had the baby, I'd be alone."

Solving the problems that contribute to the demand for abortion will not be easy. The two obvious components are: preventing unwanted pregnancies in the first place, and assisting women who . . . become pregnant anyway.

When I asked, "Is there anything anyone could have done? What would you have needed in order to have had the child?"

I heard the same answer over and over: "I needed a friend. I felt so alone. I felt like I didn't have a choice. If only one person had stood by me, even a stranger, I would have had that baby."

We also must stop thinking about abortion in terms of pregnancy. Too often we harp on pregnancy and forget all about what comes next. Getting through the pregnancy isn't nearly the dilemma that raising a child for 18 years is. In most families, marriage lightens the load, but for some people that isn't the best solution. A neglected option is adoption, which can free the woman to resume her life while giving the child a loving home.

The numbers on this, however, are shocking. Only 2 percent of unwed pregnant women choose to place their babies for adoption. Among clients at crisis-pregnancy centers, it's 1 to 2 percent.

Adoption is a difficult sell to make for a number of complex reasons, but the bottom line is that 80 to 90 percent of the clients who go through pregnancy care centers and have their babies end by setting up single-parent homes. This is very serious. Pregnancy care centers know this but aren't sure what to do about it.

I, for one, have been strongly encouraging that there be more emphasis on presenting adoption to clients, and equipping center volunteers so they feel comfortable with the topic and enabled to discuss it. Adoption is not a one-size-fits-all solution, but it's got to fit more than 1 or 2 percent. More women should try it on for size.

A case for common cause

In the abortion debate, people are suspicious of looking for any kind of common ground with their adversaries. Why should prolife partisans—or prochoicers, for that matter, who feel as strongly about their position as I do about mine—meet together in dialogue? Why should we have anything to do with each other, when the stakes are so high and the convictions so deep?

But common ground does not mean compromise. Compromise is not possible; the alternatives are too stark. Common ground does not have to do with meticulous negotiation whereby, for example, one side gives up partial-birth abortions while the other side gives up RU-486.

In this case, common ground means something more like a demilitarized zone, a safe space where conversation and exploration can take place. It can also refer to those unexpected areas of overlap where both sides find they agree. Imagine two overlapping circles of conviction, one prolife and one prochoice. Each circle is complete and has integrity. But there is a space of overlap where beliefs actually coincide—for example, that no one should be forced to have an abortion against her will.

I have been involved in the Common Ground Network for Life and Choice for five years, and can only bear witness from my own life. In light of the deadlocked, rancorous, poisonous quality of much of this debate, the appearance of Common Ground has been a healing, hopeful experience for me. And I dare hope that one day we may actually see solutions.

Common Ground is, at root, people talking. It's been a spontaneous impulse arising in a dozen cities or so across the country over the last six or seven years: Denver, Buffalo, Cleveland, Washington. Eventually the various groups linked up through an umbrella organization we call the Common Ground Network for Life and Choice, with Washington headquarters.

While Common Ground isn't for everyone, I believe it is a movement that promises to season the abortion debate with patience, consideration, and respect—something the present mudwrestling sorely needs.

One of the reasons why I participate in Common Ground is curiosity. Don't you ever wonder, "What are those people on the other side thinking? What makes them tick?" In our local group, we take turns asking questions like, "Will contraception and sex education reduce the numbers of abortions?" and "What are the acceptable limits of protest outside of abortion clinics?" In fact, two Common Grounders, an Operation Rescue leader and the administrator of an abortion clinic, are planning to write a joint paper on that very question.

Another sort of curiosity is born of frustration. I am frustrated by the deadlock on this issue, by the intractability of it, and simply want to take a crack at coming at it from a new angle—like the toddler sitting at a computer keyboard and thinking, "I wonder what will happen if I push this button?"

Sometimes, just trying something new because you're frustrated with the old can lead to disaster. But I cannot see any danger in Common Ground dialogues. Prolifers, at least, have nothing to lose, because we have nothing: the status quo lies with the other side, with court decisions to hold it in place.

Again and again, I learned that women had abortions because they felt abandoned—they felt isolated and afraid.

Through my participation in Common Ground, I also hope to eliminate misunderstanding and replace it with genuine disagreement.

I'm not naive enough to believe that our divisions are superficial, and that if we could only chat them away it would be all hugs and kisses. But misunderstanding—genuine confusion about what your opponent believes and what motivates her—is a waste of time.

I know I get weary of being told I'm prolife because I'm sexist, or antisex, or want women to be restricted to breeding and not allowed to have careers or carry cell phones. This fantasy is untrue. If prochoicers truly understood what motivates me, I don't think they would like it much better, but at least they would not be going on bogeyman stories.

Likewise, prochoicers must get weary of being told they're "proabortion" because it makes them so much money, that they don't care about children and families, and are elite godless commie pinko perverts to boot. I'd like to diffuse our absurd misunderstandings, so we can get down to grappling with the honest disagreements underneath.

Facts worth finding

I also like to talk about a related point I call data block versus ideo block. Sometimes our conflict is honestly based in different beliefs or ideologies: we are looking at the same reality (for example, the abortion of an infant with Down's syndrome) and simply disagree about what constitutes right or wrong.

In other cases, however, we disagree about what the facts are in the first place—our communication is experiencing a data block, not an ideology block.

One side, for example, tends to believe that better sex education and access to contraception will reduce the numbers of abortions. The other side tends to believe that, under a principle of unintended consequences, these items actually increase the likelihood of unwed pregnancy.

Which is true? Each side can marshal a barrage of facts to support its theory, but it's like swimming in soup—too many details, not enough certainty.

If one theory or the other could be proved true, the dissenting side might be persuaded. Both sides are looking for ways to reduce the numbers of abortions; we have a shared goal. We're just in disagreement about whether contraception will get us there, because we're holding different sets of facts.

One project the Common Ground Network has discussed is establishing a data bank of facts that both sides agree on. We could start with basics: how many abortions per year or when the fetal heartbeat begins. Trickier questions we could refer to organizations on both sides of the issue—and whenever we discover agreement, we could add it to the list. Gradually a data bank could grow, which would serve as a resource to journalists, students, and other researchers and contribute to clearing the air. A glossary might also be useful.

Common Ground allows us to scout out areas far from the hot center, where agreement may already exist. We've found, for example, a common interest in making adoption a more accessible option and raising the profile of that alternative. We've agreed on the urgency of reducing unwed teen pregnancy, and that it's wrong to use violence outside of clinics.

By continually putting our heads together in Common Ground, I keep hoping we'll find fresh ways of understanding the problem. I hope that informal and friendly links forged across the great divide can grow, over time, from rope bridges to giant trestles linking continents. But even now the power of networking is astonishing. All of us together have resources that neither of us has alone.

A few years ago, for example, the Reproductive Health Services clinic in St. Louis, Missouri was faced with an extremely young client who was too far along to have an abortion. This girl needed to be on complete bed rest to safely finish her pregnancy and needed someone to stay with her all day while her mother worked.

The clinic did not have the resources to collect a roster of volunteers for this duty. The clinic administrator, a member of the local Common Ground group, then phoned a prolifer in the group, a woman who had been arrested leading protests outside the clinic. The prolifer was able to enlist a cohort of volunteers from the prolife community, and the girl was able to safely complete her pregnancy.

If the prochoice and prolife communities had been locked in the sort of armed warfare seen in most cities, the side that had the resources—in this case, the prolife side—might never have known that the other side had a need. The more we get to know each other, the more suspicious fear can evaporate, and the more likely we are to find opportunities to actually make a difference.

Now it's personal

Being in Common Ground has eased my heart. I have found that having a prochoicer listen intently to my beliefs, then repeat them back to me accurately, is healing.

I believe I now have a much better understanding of how things stand from the prochoice point of view, too. My views haven't changed; I still believe that their position is wrong. But my listening, for example, has taught me how much a phrase like "abortion kills babies" hurts many who hold a prochoice position. To prolifers, it's just a forceful statement of fact; but I've discovered that prochoicers almost inevitably hear, "I think you personally like killing babies." So I try to express my feelings on this without implying that those who disagree are callous or depraved. They're not. They're just wrong.

Likewise, the phrase "antichoice" hits me like a slap in the face. I'm not easily angered, but being called "antichoice" makes me see red. Yes, I don't believe that taking a life is an appropriate private choice. But when I'm called "antichoice," I feel like I'm being told I'm a fascist, and that if I had my way people wouldn't be allowed to choose anything—hair color, make of car, what they'll have for supper. I think my prochoice friends, who use it interchangeably with "antiabortion" and "prolife," probably don't realize how it stings. Seeing things from the other's point of view is one of the advantages of dialogue.

When I'm called "antichoice," I feel like I'm being told I'm a fascist, and that if I had my way people wouldn't be allowed to choose anything—hair color, make of car, what they'll have for supper.

I also participate in Common Ground because I am committed to a consistent ethic of valuing all human life and rejecting violence as a means of solving social problems. Cardinal Joseph Bernardin, of blessed memory, gave the nation a gift when he defined the moral principle that underlies this ethic as a "seamless garment": the consistent opposition to war, abortion, and capital punishment. Not all prolifers view these three forms of death-dealing as morally equivalent, but it's the view that appeals most to me. In any case, all prolifers would say that abortion is the most urgent of these three, the only one taking 4,000 lives a day in this country.

As I root out of my life a spirit of violence at deeper and deeper levels, I come face to face with Jesus' command to love my enemies. It's because I've uncovered a startling fact: it wasn't until I became a prolife activist that, for the first time in my life, I had actual enemies. Realizing that I had them, I knew then what I had to do—after all, the scriptural instruction on this is not vague.

I also think of another scripture passage, the one that says you cannot love your brother whom you have not seen. So I think that's the least I can do: to go see them, on a regular basis. True, the Common Ground movement is not the sort that sweeps the country, generating TV ads, political candidates, Hollywood parties, and T-shirt slogans. But it's the sort of movement that, I hope, can begin to subtly disrupt entrenched patterns of mistrust and loathing.

If prolifers and prochoicers ripped off the scary masks we've imposed on each other, we would discover that underneath there are sincere people who, astonishingly, have the same goal: reducing the heartbreakingly high number of abortions. Both know that 4,000 abortions a day is too many. We can harness that agreement for positive change, leaving those areas where we disagree for action within our own sides.

10

Late-Term Abortion Is Unjustifiable

John F. Kavanaugh

John F. Kavanaugh, a Jesuit priest, teaches at Saint Louis University. He is author of Following Christ in a Consumer Society, Faces of Poverty, *and* Faces of Christ.

Photographs of unborn babies in the third trimester of development—which show fully developed human features—prove without a shadow of a doubt that these babies are human beings. Therefore, abortions conducted during the third trimester of pregnancy are homicides and cannot be justified.

There were two groups conspicuously absent from the State of the Union Address, 2000. The first was nine Supreme Court justices. Our most judicious body seems to have had a case of the collective flu. The other absent group was third-trimester unborn human beings. These groups will face each other when the court examines the attempts to protect the lives of the latter.

As for the speech itself, despite its litany of proposals for justice, equality, help for "kids," child care, Hillary Clinton's "tireless work" for children and families over 30 years, "the gun death rate of children" and "saving millions of lives," there was no talk of the unborn child—this despite the fact that President Clinton has clearly linked the much desired election of his vice-president with his assurance that any partial-birth abortion bill will be vetoed.

I fell asleep during the first 15 minutes but read the text the next day in the *New York Times*. It seemed like a huge bribe to me. Things so dear to my own commitments—more equitable distribution of wealth, concern for global poverty, a truly living wage, tax cuts for the middle class, more effective health care for all, greater commitment to education—were dangled before me, if only I would forget the absent constituency of which my conscience keeps reminding me. Try as I might to be seduced by the cornucopia of promises, I could not forget an image.

The December 1999 issue of *Life* magazine, with three Wise Men bending before the Child on the cover, featured an article that is only possibly a devastating rebuke of our national policy. "Born Twice" begins with a vivid, glowing picture of a womb outside the pregnant mother's body. Reaching through an incision in the uterus is a human arm, the length of a grown-up's hand, its own hand a little larger than the doctor's finger it was holding.

A living patient

Forget all theological commitment. Ignore philosophical speculation. Just look at the evidence. This is a patient. A living patient. Let no sophist tell you that we're not sure its life has begun. It is a human's hand we see, not the paw of a hamster or the limb of a tree (although some people seem more empathetic to these than to the patient within the womb).

There are those who honestly believe that a human life does not begin at conception. Others think that a human life cannot begin until there is a human brain. Those of us who disagree ethically, theologically and scientifically with such judgments may still respect them while contesting them.

But unborn third-trimester humans are another story. If you think the patient reaching out her hand from the womb is anything other than a human being, you are either a fool, a liar or (one in charity may hope) a victim of illusion and cultural group-think.

I'm sorry if that last paragraph is offensive to some of our readers. So be it. This is a time to offend and be offended.

Fetal surgery on Sarah Marie Switzer, when she was a 24-week-old fetus with spina bifida, was surgery on a human being. You may want to argue the niceties of calling such a fetus a "person," as Peter Singer and others do—and you will, with them, soon deny such personhood to infants, toddlers, the handicapped and the brain-damaged. And you will reap the whirlwind. But you cannot deny these patients their living humanity, "the most important fact of our life," our president so touchingly put it.

Third-trimester abortions are homicides. Some people argue that such homicides are justified to save a mother's life. But do they really think homicide is justified for "health?" Will they, with Singer et al., propose infanticide on the same grounds as well? Will they recommend forced euthanasia for those who burden us?

Stepping into a moral abyss

With the legal sanction of third-trimester abortions, we have not started on some moral slippery slope. We have stepped into an abyss. The concocters of Roe v. Wade seem to have suspected as much. Even though they could "not resolve the difficult question of when life begins" (if Sarah Marie Switzer was not living, was she dead when they operated on her?), they knew there was damning and incontrovertible evidence available at 24 weeks.

"With respect to the state's important and legitimate interest in potential life, the 'compelling' point is at viability. This is so because the fetus presumably has the capability of meaningful life outside the mother's womb. State regulation of fetal life after viability thus has both logical and biological justifications. If the state is interested in protecting fetal life after viability, it may go so far as to proscribe abortion during that period except when it is necessary to preserve the life or health of the mother. . . ."

Third-trimester abortions are homicides.

In the coming months we will witness what this high court of our nation's conscience deems "necessary" to kill unborn but indubitably living human "patients." Should they throw their fate upon the not so tender mercies of "choice," I will more than grieve our contempt for the unborn.

I recoil from the thought of a presidential candidate who, with Jesus as his "political inspiration," has made a reputation for overseeing executions in the state of Texas. I will not abet the policies of "America first," labor last and the poor of the world lost. But I also know this: So soured is my stomach at the thought of another president who vetoes any protection for third-trimester patients, I will have no part of any group that wins a presidency at the cost of those patients' lives and our consciences.

11

Late-Term Abortion Is Sometimes Justifiable

Ellen Goodman

Ellen Goodman is a syndicated columnist.

The effort to ban late-term abortion—which is the pro-life movement's most recent attempt to end all forms of legal abortion—is based on falsehoods. Women who seek late-term abortions do not do so out of irresponsibility or convenience, as antiabortion groups suggest. In truth, a late-term abortion is only conducted when it is necessary to protect life and health of the mother.

At least they won't be showing the cartoon in the Supreme Court. For once we will hold this debate without the infamous line drawings that look straight through a woman, as if she were an invisible vessel, to the perfect Gerber baby lying within.

That's been the defining image, the most graphic of graphics ever since the pro-life movement invented the phrase "partial-birth abortion" as another strike on the public opinion front.

The Supreme Court prefers the Constitution to the cartoon. So today they'll hear a case—Stenberg vs. Carhart—that has ratcheted up the rhetoric and the politics of abortion. And with luck, the woman will not be invisible.

This wrangling over so-called "partial-birth abortion" has been on an inevitable path to the high court. Over the past decade or more, anti-abortion groups switched from trying to make abortion illegal to trying to make it impossible. While one arm attacked clinics, another created hurdles.

The propaganda about late-term abortions

Five years ago, pro-lifers embarked on a new tactic to ban abortion one procedure at a time. The first target is what's known to medicine as dilation and extraction—and the propaganda has been unrelenting. The central message is that droves of women carry their pregnancies to near term and then choose abortion instead of delivery.

The Catholic bishops first ran ads implying that a woman would have a late-term abortion to fit into her prom gown. Since then, one pro-life congressman after another, like Joe Pitts of Pennsylvania, has suggested that women would choose these abortions if they "had a bad day." Or was it a bad hair day?

Congress has repeatedly passed a ban—most recently this month—just short of veto-proof. Some 30 states have also passed similar laws, most of which were overturned.

Then last fall, the 7th Circuit Court of Appeals upheld bans almost identical to those the 8th Circuit struck down. And since women of Nebraska, Arkansas and Iowa do not get a different set of fundamental rights than women in Wisconsin and Illinois, the matter landed in the Supreme Court.

The man who challenged the Nebraska law and put his name on this case is by no means a crusader from central casting. LeRoy Carhart is a retired Air Force lieutenant colonel who chose Nebraska as the place to practice medicine, and raise his family and his horses. But, at 58, he is also part of that diminishing breed of doctors who actually remember when abortion was illegal. He saw the results.

Today Dr. Carhart is the only remaining doctor in Nebraska who does second-trimester abortions. His patients have included preteen girls, women with cancer, diabetes, heart disease, AIDS.

The truth about late-term abortions

All of these abortions were performed before the fetus was viable. Indeed, contrary to the spin on this story, "partial-birth abortion" bans are not truly directed at third trimester or viable fetuses. Such abortions are already banned by Nebraska and, indeed, by Roe vs. Wade, except to protect the life and health of the woman.

"Partial-birth abortion" bans are not truly directed at third trimester or viable fetuses. Such abortions are already banned.

"Women's health became my life," Dr. Carhart has said. It's cost him his home and his horses—victims to arsonists who linked their violence to his work. When the pro-life state legislature passed the ban, Dr. Carhart realized that the wording was purposely broad enough to threaten any doctor using a range of safe, common methods. The penalty was, after all, 20 years in prison. That's twice the penalty for performing an illegal abortion in the bad old days.

There are a number of reasons to predict the Supreme Court will rule against these deep incursions into abortion rights. The words "partial-birth abortion" have no fixed meaning in medicine; the laws are so vague that a doctor would have to guess which methods are outlawed. The lawmakers are also practicing medicine without a license, deciding which treatment a doctor can and cannot provide.

But the most insidious part of the campaign is that these laws make no allowance to protect the health of the woman.

The Nebraska ban, like the ones before Congress, only permits an exception to save her life. Do we really want a pro-life legislator to have the second and final opinion? Do we want the state to decide when and which abortion is necessary to save the life of the woman? And when it is merely to save her uterus, her kidney, her eyesight?

The most insidious part of the campaign [to ban late-term abortions] is that these laws make no allowance to protect the health of the woman.

And do we think for a minute that if the ban on this procedure holds, there won't be another ban? And another?

Keep in mind that cartoon portrait. Another unlikely source, Judge Richard Posner, a conservative Reagan-appointed appeals court judge, has probably written the best caption. In a blistering opinion he wrote that the "partial-birth abortion" bans are only concerned with making a statement in the ongoing war for public opinion: "The statement is that fetal life is more valuable than women's health."

It's up to the Supreme Court now to put the woman back in the picture.

12

Aborting a Handicapped Fetus Is Unethical

Paul Greenberg

Paul Greenberg is the editorial page editor of the Little Rock Democrat-Gazette *and a nationally syndicated columnist.*

With recent advances in prenatal screening, many unborn babies found to have Down syndrome are aborted. Society is proceeding down a slippery slope to the use of abortion to get rid of "imperfect" babies. The legalization of abortion has helped create a society that regards death as an acceptable solution to life's problems.

Here's something to remember the next time the name of Joycelyn Elders, former surgeon general and lightning rod, is affixed to another honor roll, hall of fame or list of endorsements for a candidate or condom: Why not add some memorable quotation from her body of wit and wisdom, some gem of philosophy to go with her official portrait? Much like the brief quotes that used to appear under the pictures of graduating seniors in any respectable high school annual.

But which quotation? The good doctor has said so many things one can't forget (as much as you might like to) that it would be hard to choose just the right one. Yet one of her observations does stand out in memory—like a bright, shining beacon that illuminates the dark road ahead.

The statement was made a couple of years ago—even before partial-birth abortions were being touted at the country's medical schools, even before appellate courts were opening the doors to euthanasia, and perhaps even before Dr. Kevorkian was being hailed as a savior who only wanted to ease our suffering—even if the side effects might include death. The statement came during her testimony before the Senate Labor and Human Resources Committee, as Dr. Elders was saying, once again, that "abortion has had an important, and positive, public-health effect."

How's that? Well, the good doctor explained, "the number of Down syndrome infants in Washington state in 1976 was 64 percent lower than it would have been without legal abortion."

Reprinted from Paul Greenberg, "Perfect Babies via Abortion," *Arizona Republic*, April 3, 1996. Reprinted with permission from the author.

Isn't it wonderful to have brought down the rate of Down syndrome births by so dramatic a margin? Gosh, how could the state of Washington have achieved so striking a scientific advance?

Think about it.

Of course. The doctors simply aborted a large number of babies/fetuses found to have Down, thus keeping down the cost of health care and raising the general Quality of Life. And the only thing this marked gain in public health cost was life itself.

The perfect baby syndrome

Dr. Elders' comment foreshadowed the latest development in our ever-expanding culture of death: the revival of eugenics, the science of human breeding. Call it the Perfect Baby Syndrome. Because with the new advances in prenatal testing it becomes more and more possible to eliminate any feature of your baby that disturbs—simply by eliminating the baby.

The slippery slope only starts with Down syndrome. There are so many other problems, handicaps, conditions, and deviations from the statistical mean that can now be eliminated early—long before any personal attachments may get in the way. Spina bifida, for example. Or hydrocephalus.

Of course there will always be those who stand in the way of progress. A columnist for the London Spectator, for example, had written about how much his daughter, a Down baby, had come to mean to him. In turn his column evoked this letter to the Spectator's editor:

With the new advances in prenatal testing it becomes more and more possible to eliminate any feature of your baby that disturbs—simply by eliminating the baby.

"I have severe spina bifida and am a full-time wheelchair user. I also run the Handicap Division of the Society for the Protection of Unborn Children—a group of disabled people. It is difficult for me to express my appreciation of your positive, loving attitude toward your daughter, since it means so much to me. I feel that your acceptance embraces all disabled people, and it represents such a radically different view to the one more commonly expressed. Every day I read in the press about 'exciting breakthroughs,' which mean yet another way to kill people like me before birth. . . ."

In a society in which no reason need be given for an abortion, why cavil about a way of lowering the rate of children born with Down? Why not think of it, to quote Dr. Elders, as an "important, and positive, public-health effect"? Just imagine the Important and Positive Public-Health Effects to come. ("Tired of having brown-eyed boys in the family? Want to try for a blue-eyed girl instead?") Even now amniocentesis isn't used just to satisfy the prospective parents' idle curiosity.

A brave new, and uniform, world

As the genetic map is decoded, all kinds of wondrous/horrific possibilities present themselves—like Mephistopheles with a deal you can't refuse. What a brave new, and uniform, world it could be. A world without Down and spina bifida and dyslexia and color-blindedness and allergies and left-handedness and . . .

The possibilities are as endless as death itself. Roe v. Wade stands like an open gate to this beckoning future of the Perfect Baby. Entrance is free to anybody who doesn't think too long or too hard. Or who just tends to follow Fashion, or Science or Authority without asking too many questions.

Roe v. Wade stands like an open gate to [the] beckoning future of the Perfect Baby.

Richard John Neuhaus is editor-in-chief of *First Things* magazine, a thoroughly subversive influence in pagan America. He reports regularly on the unfolding Culture of Death, and it seems to be advancing from both ends of life's spectrum toward the middle. Roe v. Wade only cracked the door. Now an appellate decision out of the 9th Circuit Court has cited Roe as the basis of a constitutional right to suicide/hastened death—with or without the patient's explicit permission.

Perhaps the most arresting phrase of this pro-death ruling may have been an almost offhand observation in the majority opinion: "The slippery slope fears of Roe's opponents have, of course, not materialized." Of course not. Only a million and a half perfectly legal abortions are performed in this country every year, the organ-harvesting industry grows in tandem with abortion, and euthanasia is now getting a new lease on death. Moral: There is no denial of the slippery slope quite so impressive as one that comes from a court already a good way down it.

13

Aborting a Handicapped Fetus Is Ethical

Ann Bradley

Ann Bradley is a writer for Living Marxism, *a British magazine that covers a variety of cultural, moral, medical, and scientific issues.*

It is not unethical for a woman to choose to abort a handicapped fetus. Because the woman would be responsible for raising the handicapped child, only she can decide whether to bring the pregnancy to term. The theoretical "interests of the fetus" do not outweigh the real rights of the mother.

These days there is not much support for anti-abortion arguments *per se.* Even old-fashioned moralists like Victoria Gillick hesitate before saying that women should be prevented from having abortions—they prefer to argue that such women are damaged victims of a promiscuous society. But once the issue of fetal handicap is raised, everything seems to change.

Many pro-choice activists who defend women's right to end accidental, unwanted pregnancies gag when asked if a woman should be able to terminate a pregnancy—not because she does not wish to have a child, but because she does not want to have a *disabled* child. Indeed even many of those who lobby for abortion on request in early pregnancy see late abortion on the grounds of fetal handicap as a form of discrimination against disabled people—'disability cleansing'. This makes it a perfect issue for the anti-abortion lobby to take up. There is little ground for them to gain in arguing against early abortion, which is now acceptable to the overwhelming majority of people. But when the antis take the argument into the territory of late abortion on the grounds of fetal handicap they find that even many pro-choice activists are prepared to make concessions.

Allowing a healthy woman to have an abortion purely on the grounds that her fetus is handicapped smacks of a number of things which many liberals find unacceptable. It is judgmental and value-laden because, in opting to end the pregnancy, the woman says that while she

Reprinted from Ann Bradley, "Why Shouldn't Women Abort Disabled Fetuses?" *Living Marxism*, September 1995. Reprinted with permission from *Living Marxism*.

was keen to raise an able child she is not prepared to raise a disabled one. In deciding to abort an abnormal fetus a woman is clearly saying that although she wanted a child, she does not want one on the terms that nature has offered. There are many who find it difficult to accept that some women should seek to take control of their own destiny at the expense of a handicapped fetus.

A hotly debated issue

Even members of the medical profession now say that they are finding the moral issue 'difficult' to resolve, especially with developments in fetal medicine which allow, and encourage, doctors to take action in respect of a fetus. For some doctors, these developments have led to the perception that the fetus is a patient like any other and the subject of medical intervention in its own right. It may be difficult for doctors to accept that, while they are struggling to maintain fetal life at 28 weeks gestation on one day, they can be called upon to end it on the next. The Royal College of Obstetricians and Gynaecologists has commissioned a working party to make specific recommendations on the issue of abortion on the grounds of fetal handicap, and it is being hotly debated in the pages of respected medical journals. Already this year the prestigious *British Journal of Obstetrics and Gynaecology* has carried two articles calling for a reassessment of current abortion law in accordance with changed views on disability.

In June 1995, three eminent professors argued that once the fetus is viable (ie, once extra-uterine life could be sustained, if necessary with the aid of technology—usually accepted to be 24 weeks gestation), it should be considered a patient in its own right and one towards which the doctor has a 'beneficence-based responsibility'. These three very eminent professors argue that abortion in the third trimester should be ethically impermissible, unless the fetus has a serious abnormality that can be diagnosed with certainty and which involves an early death or absence of cognitive developmental capacity. This would rule out abortion for conditions such as Down's Syndrome or spina bifida, where neither death nor absence of cognitive developmental capacity can be defined as a certain or near certain outcome.

The acceptance of the fetus as a patient in its own right to which the doctor had specific obligations would be significant, because it would attribute a form of personhood to the fetus, something which it does not yet possess in British law. Although the notion is creeping into American legal definitions, it has been resisted by the British medico-legal establishment for very good reasons.

The fetus cannot possess autonomy

Even after it reaches the 24-week stage of viability, the fetus does not have a life of its own independent from the woman who carries it. The fetus cannot be understood to possess 'autonomy'. However, actions taken in the supposed 'interests of the fetus' may well infringe the very real autonomy of the woman carrying it. Such actions may even cause her serious harm if they involve clinical intervention against her wishes, or the denial of clinical intervention that she requests—such as an abortion. Few British doctors or legal experts want to be in the position of some of their American colleagues in presiding over forced Caesarean deliveries, or dealing with cases where pregnant women have been imprisoned to prevent them acting in such a way as to possibly harm the fetus.

So far, the majority of medical opinion in the UK has clung to the notion that it is impossible to separate the interests of the fetus *in utero* from those of the pregnant woman because any decisions taken in respect of the fetus will necessarily affect her. This is as true after viability as before. Doctors treat the fetus at the request of, and on behalf of, the pregnant woman. Consequently when making decisions about late abortions for fetal handicap, most sympathetic doctors act in the declared interests of the woman—the interests of the fetus do not really enter into it.

This is exactly as it should be. It is the woman, after all, who has to take responsibility for the child after it has been born, and so only she is in a position to determine whether or not she is able or prepared to take the strain involved in rearing a severely handicapped child. And the overwhelming majority of women who discover that they are carrying a fetus affected by Down's Syndrome currently choose to have an abortion.

Only [the woman] is in a position to determine whether or not she is able or prepared to take the strain involved in rearing a severely handicapped child.

A study by antenatal screening expert Professor Eva Alberman shows that just eight per cent of women who discover they are carrying a fetus affected by Down's Syndrome decide to continue the pregnancy. And, many would argue, for good reason. When a woman decides to have a child she has an image of what motherhood will be like and what her child will be like. A severely handicapped child—whatever perspective it has on me—simply is not what she anticipated or wanted. Access to antenatal testing and the option of abortion allows a woman to make an informed decision about the future of her pregnancy—and about her own future.

Why should a woman in this situation be denied the option of ending the pregnancy in abortion? No one, at least in this country, argues that women who wish to have disabled children should have their pregnancies forcibly aborted. The argument centres on whether a woman should be allowed to decide whether to continue a pregnancy which she now finds unacceptable.

A slippery slope?

Those who campaign against abortion argue that women's choice should be denied because the acceptance of abortion for fetal handicap has a corrosive effect on society. They argue that termination for fetal handicap is a slippery slope to euthanasia for the living handicapped, and that by condoning abortion on these grounds society condones discrimination against handicapped people. But this inexorable logic rests on the assumption that we are incapable of differentiating between our actions in respect of fetuses—potential people—and people themselves. After all, those who believe that abortion is a legitimate end to unwanted pregnancy do not accept infanticide as a way of dealing with unwanted babies or murder as a way of disposing of an unwanted partner. The point about slippery slopes—as John Harris, one of Britain's few professors in ethics with his feet on the ground, puts it—is that we, like skiers, learn to negotiate them.

There is much intense speculation about the quality of life of the disabled, and it is this issue which seems to confuse many members of the medical profession. If a fetus is disabled in such a way that the child will endure a short life of intense pain, then it is more likely that there will be a consensus that abortion is legitimate. Things are seen as less clear-cut if the fetal problem is such that the child, were it to be born, would be able to live with a mental handicap which made it unaware that it was even different from other children. But this argument is only of relevance if you assess the legitimacy of abortion from the point of view of the fetus, rather than that of the pregnant woman who may be less willing to assume responsibility for mental handicap than physical pain. If one assumes that a woman should be able to act on what is right for *her* rather than what is right for the fetus—which is not sentient, conscious or aware that there is such a thing as life or death—then this argument loses all validity.

Those who oppose abortion for fetal abnormality have been allowed to assume the moral high ground in the discussion. It is assumed that in an ideal world no woman would want to abort an abnormal fetus—we would accept the diversity they bring. Even many of those who will accept abortion on grounds of handicap often concede a moral superiority to those who, like [*Spectator* editor] Dominic Lawson, accept the birth of a child with Down's Syndrome or spina bifida with the same joy as a normal baby. Many of those who wrote to the papers disagreeing with Lawson's line made clear that they saw abortion as an appropriate option only for those who are 'unable to meet the challenge of disability', or accept their child's 'special talents', in the way that an 'enlightened parent' like Lawson could.

Access to antenatal testing and the option of abortion allows a woman to make an informed decision about the future of her pregnancy—and about her own future.

Yet why should those who opt for abortion be made to feel that their decision is a symptom of their weakness and lack of moral fibre? Many of the correspondents eulogising about Lawson seemed to display a peculiar perversity in assuming that a mental handicap confers special advantages on a child and its parents. Former feminist campaigner, Erin Pizzey, shared with readers of the *Spectator* her experience that those with

Down's Syndrome were 'without exception magic children. . . . What those extra genes did was to enable them to give unconditional love'. Another correspondent suggested that those with Down's Syndrome are 'stars in an increasingly materialistic world':

'Those of us with a Down's Syndrome child (our son, Robert, is almost 24) often wish that all our children had this extraordinary syndrome which deletes anger and malice, replacing them with humour, thoughtfulness and devotion to friends and family.'

Think about what is really being said here. The argument appears to be that it is preferable to have the unconditional love and unconscious devotion of a mentally handicapped child/adult than it is to have to earn the love and respect of someone who is potentially/actually your equal. Where is the moral superiority in that? If unconditional love and uncritical devotion is what you want, you would arguably be better advised to forget about people altogether and get a puppy.

Access to abortion on request

Those who argue that the current abortion law is riddled with eugenic assumptions undeniably have a point. The law was constructed on the assumption that abortion should be available in circumstances where doctors believe that a woman's capacity for good motherhood is undermined by her health or her circumstances, or that it would be better for society if her child were not born. The current abortion law is not the kind of law that women need. We need access to abortion on request—for whatever reason *we* think is appropriate. But until we have won such a law it is important to defend the access to abortion that current legislation gives us— including access to late abortion for fetal handicap—and to celebrate rather than condemn the use of medical technology that allows women the chance to make a choice.

14

Research Using Human Embryos Is Morally Acceptable

Peter Singer

Peter Singer, an ethics scholar and supporter of animal rights, is the author of Animal Liberation, Practical Ethics, How Are We to Live?, *and* Rethinking Life and Death. *He is DeCamp Professor of Bioethics at the University Center for Human Values at Princeton University.*

The undifferentiated cells of a human embryo—often referred to as "stem cells"—hold limitless promise for medical research. Theoretically, such cells could cure leukemia, treat diseases such as Parkinson's and Alzheimer's, and repair the nerve systems of quadriplegics. Abortion opponents, however, are attempting to ban stem cell research on the grounds that it is unethical. This is untrue. There is no reason to object to research conducted on a being that has no brain, consciousness, preferences of any kind, or capacity for suffering.

When a human embryo consists of not more than 64 cells, its cells are, like a young dog, able to learn new tricks. If injected into a diseased kidney, they take on many of the properties of ordinary kidney cells, and may help the kidney to perform its normal function. This seems to hold for any organ, even any kind of cell. This is exciting medical researchers, because it means that, at least in theory, the cells from an early embryo could cure leukemia, enable people with diabetes to manufacture insulin, treat Parkinson's and Alzheimer's disease, and repair the nerve systems of quadriplegics.

But medical researchers aren't the only ones excited by the prospects of using embryo stem cells. In the United States, 70 members of Congress have opposed a proposal from the National Institutes of Health, the major government funding body for medical research, to sponsor work using human stem cells. The National Conference of Catholic Bishops has lobbied Congress to prevent the use of federal funding for the research, and when a coalition called Patients' Cure began to campaign for embryo

Reprinted from Peter Singer, "Stem Cells and Immortal Souls," *Free Inquiry*, Spring 2000. Reprinted with permission from *Free Inquiry*.

stem cell research, Cardinal William Keeler of Baltimore wrote to the American Cancer Society, a sponsor of Patients' Cure, to urge it to reconsider its position. The American Cancer Society withdrew its support from Patients' Cure.

Opposition to research on human embryos

Opponents of research on human embryos usually start and finish their argument with the claim that the human embryo is, from the moment of conception, a living, innocent human being. But the morality of using a being for research should depend on what the being is like, not on the species to which it belongs. Other things being equal, there is less reason for objecting to the use of an early human embryo—a being that has no brain, is not, and never has been conscious, and has no preferences of any kind—than there is for objecting to research on rats, who are sentient beings capable of preferring not to be in situations that are painful or frightening to them. (Note the qualification "other things being equal." If the people from whom the egg and sperm were obtained would be distressed to know that an embryo conceived from these gametes was used in experimentation, that would be a reason why it might be wrong to do so. The same would be true if the experiments were badly designed, and so used scarce research funds for no good purpose.)

The cells from an early embryo could cure leukemia, enable people with diabetes to manufacture insulin, treat Parkinson's and Alzheimer's disease, and repair the nerve systems of quadriplegics.

Opposition to the use of embryo stem cells comes overwhelmingly from those with a religious viewpoint: they believe that embryos have immortal souls, and that is why they are worthy of greater protection than nonhuman animals. If people who hold these beliefs are successful in preventing research on embryo stem cells in the United States, they will merely have demonstrated the extent to which nonreligious citizens of the United States continue to be disadvantaged by the strength of religious belief in this country.

An embryo cannot suffer

Research on embryos should be prohibited if there is any possibility that the embryo is capable of suffering—but no one would argue that an embryo consisting of 64 cells could be capable of suffering. A developed brain and nervous system is a pre-requisite for a capacity to suffer. Apart from belief in immortal souls, it is sheer species-bias that makes us permit all kinds of trivial uses to be made of sentient nonhumans, and then prevents much research that is far more significant from being carried out because it requires cells from early, nonsentient human embryos.

15

Research Using Human Embryos Is Morally Unacceptable

Russell E. Saltzman

Russell E. Saltzman is the pastor of Christ Lutheran Church in Stover, Missouri, and editor of Forum Letter, *an independent Lutheran publication.*

Stem cells—cell tissue extracted from human embryos—could potentially provide an endless supply of healthy cells that could be used to regenerate damaged organs. The use of aborted embryos for this or any other purpose is an example of science taken beyond ethical limits. An embryo is a human life, not a piece of research material. From a moral standpoint, it is unacceptable for people to destroy innocent human life for their own benefit.

Remember the story of the guy who died in the flood? A Red Cross boat had come by earlier when the water was above the window sills, but the fellow refused rescue saying, "The Lord will save me." A second boat came when the water was to the eaves and the man was hanging from the gutters. But again he refused rescue. "The Lord will save me," he declared. Scrambling onto his roof ahead of the ever-rising waters the man spied a helicopter heading his way. A rope was lowered from the copter, but the obstinate guy batted it away and shouted over the din of the rotors, "The Lord will save me." Of course he drowned. He arrived at Heaven's throne perplexed, hurt, angry, and dripping wet. "Why," he shouted at God, "didn't you save me?" "Give me a break," sighed the Lord God Almighty. "I sent two boats and a helicopter."

I am a diabetic, Type II. I flunked a health insurance examination in March 1995. That's how I found out. Six months before, an annual health exam said I was as fit as I could be, for a man my age. (Doctors always add that part.) But somewhere on the inclined plane to forty-eight, my pancreas decided to malfunction and it stopped producing enough insulin to keep my blood sugar count within normal range. All of a sudden, my blood count was hitting the 400 mark. That's somewhere just short of the

Reprinted from Russell E. Saltzman, "Two Boats, a Helicopter, and Stem Cells," *First Things*, October 1999. Reprinted with permission from *First Things*.

point where you either go blind or tank out in a coma. A blood count of 80 to 120 an hour after eating is considered normal. I guess I was lucky. Of the nation's diabetics, so estimates go, only about half have been diagnosed.

Since becoming a diabetic I'm more aware of other diabetics. It seems, in fact, I can't get away from them. For most of my whole life I knew only one diabetic, a fellow up in Nebraska, but now I know literally dozens. I'm sure I knew others before, but now that my awareness has been sensitized, suddenly they're all over the place, and it seems they are losing body parts. There's Frank, age seventy. Doctors took off his lower left leg earlier this year. His trouble began with bypass surgery a year before. Any kind of surgery can be serious trouble for a diabetic. We have trouble healing. The blood doesn't travel quite as fast or as far as it should to help mend flesh. His slow recovery led to complications. At first he was to lose only the tips of his toes. His physician took those off, but after ten days in the hospital with no appreciable sign of healing, Frank lost his leg at the knee. About six weeks ago he lost the tips of his other toes. He's a game fellow, though, traveling with a walker and a prosthesis, but traveling.

Then there's Alma, eighty-three. She has lost both legs, the last of a series of amputations that began three years ago with the loss of two toes on the left leg. She never healed and her surgeon kept cutting—toes, mid-calf, mid-thigh—until he found a place where the blood did reach and would heal the wound. Then little blisters popped up on her other leg, and the tiresome ordeal began all over again. She resisted, mightily. That last leg was her last shred of mobility and she kept it as long as possible, hopping to and fro in her room at the nursing home until the pain overwhelmed her and the blood poisoning almost killed her. Indeed, as she told me, she was hoping the blood poisoning *would* kill her, and then she could be done with this misery. It was the pain that compelled her consent. Alma has been a Type II diabetic since she was in her thirties. At an age now when she ought to be puttering around her farm house, she's propped up in a nursing home wheelchair.

Living as a diabetic

Being a diabetic at first wasn't a hard thing, except for the daily finger pricks for blood samples. My blood count was controlled by a diet of 1,400 to 1,800 calories a day, and that took care of it. I could eat a whole pie, the doctor said, just so long as I ate nothing else the entire day. I wasn't exactly overweight, but trimming down a bit seemed like a good idea. At least it did until I reached my college weight of, lo! some twenty-five years before, and then kept on losing, finally dropping down to my high school weight. I was turning back into that lanky, skinny geek all the girls loved so much. That's when the doctor said, eat more. Some of the pounds came back on and I went on oral medication, one pill a day. Now I've graduated to two medications, five pills a day, and one finger prick every morning to sample my blood count. One finger prick is progress, of a sort. Early on it had been three a day. That was the bad news, the doctor said. The good news was, I could alternate fingers. She's something of a bedside humorist, the doctor is.

A chronic illness, I am learning, is a real burden. It's the chronic part that gives it such an oppressive weight, knowing I'll never be rid of it. I have discovered a new empathy with those of my parishioners who suffer similar or worse disorders, a shared experience none of us likes. But for whatever good my illness may produce—endurance, patience, character, that stuff St. Paul wrote that sounds so nice in the abstract but requires the spirituality of a saint to comprehend—I'd just as soon have let this particular cup pass, had God given me the choice. But He didn't. So I filled out the papers for free diabetic supplies and I scan the literature touting new medications, insulin pumps, magic bullets, anything that holds some promise that I won't end up clomping around like Frank or getting myself carried to the toilet like Alma. I watch my diet, stick with the medication, and, don't doubt it, I inspect my feet every morning.

The promise of fetal stem cell therapy

There's my dilemma. There is something supposedly just over the horizon that sounds for all the world like two boats and a helicopter and if I don't grab it, maybe I'm the fool? The promise is fetal stem cell therapy.

Stem cells are cell tissue extracted from human embryos. These are marvelous little things, so researchers are saying. They can be teased into providing an endless supply of healthy cells for unhealthy organs. The cells have been "convinced" by researchers to grow into nerve cells, skin cells, heart cells—in fact, potentially all of the 210 kinds of human cells can be grown from fetal stem cells. There is even a possibility of stem cells being used to treat Down Syndrome babies in the womb. Fetal cells that have become healthy pancreatic cells might be injected into a diseased pancreas and provide a lifelong cure for diabetes. Or they might be used to treat any number of other disorders like Parkinson's and Alzheimer's. There is a whole list of things at which we might squirt stem cells if researchers have their way. Stem cells are described as the Rosetta Stone for all cell research, including cloning. Quite a claim, and it may be true. It may also be quite terrible.

Fetal stem cells presently come from two sources, abandoned embryos from fertility clinics and five-to-nine-week-old aborted fetuses. So, when this research is perfected and receives FDA approval, all I have to do to benefit from it is give up my opposition to abortion and most forms of embryonic research. Swallow a little pride, take a shot or two, whatever's called for, and pretty soon I'll be eating like a regular guy, all my body parts intact. Why, after all, should we let a perfectly good embryo, one that is not a candidate for implantation in a vacant womb, go to waste? Otherwise abandoned and unwanted, should it languish frozen on a shelf somewhere, especially when there is so much good it can do for others? Aborted fetuses are already just so much waste material. Let's be green, if that's the phrase, and recycle those little suckers for all they're worth.

Why ban stem cell research?

There may be a way to avoid abortions and embryos as a stem cell source by regressing adult cells. Take some skin cells, tease them back to their primal state, and then grow them forward to make hearts, brain matter, and a cure for diabetes. The research is only in its beginnings and far, far from complete. It may be years before anything like that approaches reality. So why wait, when, according to some researchers, fetal stem cells already have proven their potential? From a utilitarian view, the argument is unassailable.

There is for the moment, but only for the moment, a federal ban on this kind of research. There is a great deal of pressure for repeal. Naturally, the ban affects only researchers who receive federal money. There is no ban against privately funded research. Drug companies and biotech firms are getting into this big. The financial gain that would accrue from a successful and proven stem cell therapy is unimaginable, and there are financial interests with some very big imaginations at play. This is one of the arguments for lifting the federal ban on fetal cell research. Someone is going to do it, is already doing it, and all of it outside the glare of public accountability. This research had better be tucked inside a government package, sanitized by a ton of federal regulations, organized by the National Institutes of Health, all to get this thing under public control. Quick. Otherwise in some few short years we will be dealing with questions of patented life, private cloning, vats of transplantable organs, and maybe the "decanted babies" and "Bokanovskian twins" (clones in today's phrase) from *Brave New World*.

There may be a way to avoid abortions and embryos as a stem cell source by regressing adult cells.

But that is exactly what we are dealing with already. Science has once again sped beyond the ken of ethical insight. The cat is out of the bag and research is roaring ahead. Federalizing fetal stem cell research will solve nothing morally because, whether federal or commercial, it requires the destruction of human embryos and it feeds on abortion. Find another source of stem cells and the moral problem goes away. But, as mentioned, finding that source will be a much slower process. Meanwhile, present research goes on with the moral status of the embryo up for grabs—is the embryo human life or a mere bit of research material?—and it walks hand in hand with that negation of life known as a woman's right to choose.

Aldous Huxley, who wrote *Brave New World* in 1933, worried that science was being twisted all around. Where once, as with the sabbath, science was made for man, he foresaw and chillingly created in his novel a world where man is made for science. In Huxley's fictionalized world the process that turned science around was methodical and deliberate, and without moral regard. In our own world, the process going on is less tidy but no less deliberate, and with equally little moral restraint.

My answer to the moral status of the embryo or the use of aborted fetuses tends to be as simple as it is adamant. It is not right for big, strong human beings to benefit themselves by preying upon weak, little human beings. And if someone wants to suggest that stem cell therapy really is God's way of coming to rescue me from an insulin drought, well, just call me gimpy.

Organizations to Contact

The editors have compiled the following list of organizations concerned with the issues debated in this book. The descriptions are derived from materials provided by the organizations. All have publications or information available for interested readers. The list was compiled on the date of publication of the present volume; the information provided here may change. Be aware that many organizations take several weeks or longer to repond to inquiries, so allow as much time as possible.

ACLU Reproductive Freedom Project
125 Broad St., New York, NY 10004-2400
(212) 549-2500
e-mail: aclu@aclu.org • website: www.aclu.org/issues/reproduct/hmrr.html

A branch of the American Civil Liberties Union, the project coordinates efforts in litigation, advocacy, and public education to guarantee the constitutional right to reproductive choice. Its mission is to ensure that reproductive decisions will be informed, meaningful, and free of hindrance or coercion from the government. The project disseminates fact sheets, pamphlets, and editorial articles. It also publishes the quarterly newsletter *Reproductive Rights Update.*

Alan Guttmacher Institute
120 Wall St., 21st Floor, New York, NY 10005
(212) 248-1111 • fax: (212) 248-1951
e-mail: info@agi-usa.org • website: www.agi-usa.org/index.html

The institute is a reproduction research group that advocates the right to safe and legal abortion. It provides extensive statistical information on abortion and voluntary population control. Publications include the bimonthly journal *Family Planning Perspectives,* which focuses on reproductive health issues; *Preventing Pregnancy, Protecting Health: A New Look at Birth Control in the U.S.;* and the book *Sex and America's Teenagers.*

American Life League (ALL)
PO Box 1350, Stafford, VA 22555
(540) 659-4171 • fax: (540) 659-2586
e-mail: whylife@all.org • website: www.all.org

ALL promotes family values and opposes abortion. The organization monitors congressional activities dealing with pro-life issues and provides information on the physical and psychological risks of abortion. It produces educational materials, books, flyers, and programs for pro-family organizations that oppose abortion. Publications include the biweekly newsletter *Communiqué,* the bimonthly magazine *Celebrate Life,* and the weekly newsletter *Lifefax.*

Americans United for Life (AUL)
310 S. Peoria St., Suite 300, Chicago, IL 60604-3816
(312) 492-7234 • fax: (312) 492-7235
e-mail: info.aul@juno.com • website: www.unitedforlife.org

AUL promotes legislation to make abortion illegal. The organization operates a library and a legal-resource center. It publishes the quarterly newsletter *Lex Vitae*, the monthly newsletters *AUL Insights* and *AUL Forum*, and numerous booklets, including *The Beginning of Human Life* and *Fetal Pain and Abortion: The Medical Evidence*.

Catholics for a Free Choice (CFFC)
1436 U St. NW, Suite 301, Washington, DC 20009
(202) 986-6093 • fax: (202) 332-7995
website: www.cath4choice.org

CFFC supports the right to legal abortion and promotes family planning to reduce the incidence of abortion and to increase women's choice in childbearing and child rearing. It publishes the bimonthly newsletter *Conscience*, the booklet *The History of Abortion in the Catholic Church*, and the brochure *You Are Not Alone*.

Center for Bio-Ethical Reform (CBR)
PO Box 8056, Mission Hills, CA 91346
(818) 360-2477 • fax: (818) 360-2477
e-mail: cbr@cbrinfo.org • website: www.cbrinfo.org

CBR opposes legal abortion, focusing its arguments on abortion's moral aspects. Its members frequently address conservative and Christian groups throughout the United States. The center also offers training seminars on fundraising to pro-life volunteers. CBR publishes the monthly newsletter *In-Perspective* and a student training manual for setting up pro-life groups on campuses titled *How to Abortion-Proof Your Campus*. Its audiotapes include "Is the Bible Silent on Abortion?" and "No More Excuses."

Childbirth by Choice Trust
344 Bloor St. West, Suite 306
Toronto, ON M5S 3A7 Canada
(416) 961-1507 • fax: (416) 961-5771
e-mail: info@cbctrust.com • website: www.cbctrust.com/homepage.html

Childbirth by Choice Trust's goal is to educate the public about abortion and reproductive choice. It produces educational materials that aim to provide factual, rational, and straightforward information about fertility control issues. The organization's publications include the booklet *Abortion in Law, History, and Religion* and the pamphlets *Unsure About Your Pregnancy? A Guide to Making the Right Decision* and *Information for Teens About Abortion*.

Feminists for Life of America
733 15th St. NW, Suite 1100, Washington, DC 20005
(202) 737-3352
e-mail: fems4life@aol.com • website: www.feministsforlife.org

This organization is comprised of feminists united to secure the right to life, from conception to natural death, for all human beings. It believes that legal abortion exploits women. The group supports a Human Life Amendment, which would protect unborn life. Publications include the quarterly *Sisterlife*, the book *Prolife Feminism: Different Voices*, the booklet *Early Feminist Case Against Abortion*, and the pamphlet *Abortion Does Not Liberate Women*.

Human Life Foundation (HLF)
215 Lexington Ave., New York, NY 10016
(212) 685-5210 • fax: (212) 725-9793
website: www.humanlifereview.com

The foundation serves as a charitable and educational support group for individuals opposed to abortion, euthanasia, and infanticide. HLF offers financial support to organizations that provide women with alternatives to abortion. Its publications include the quarterly *Human Life Review* and books and pamphlets on abortion, bioethics, and family issues.

Human Life International (HLI)
4 Family Life Ln., Front Royal, VA 22630
(540) 635-7884 • fax: (540) 635-7363
e-mail: hli@hli.org • website: www.hli.org

HLI is a pro-life family education and research organization that opposes abortion. It offers positive alternatives to what it calls the antilife/antifamily movement. The organization publishes *Confessions of a Prolife Missionary, Deceiving Birth Controllers,* and the monthly newsletters *HLI Reports* and *Special Reports.*

National Abortion and Reproductive Rights Action League (NARAL)
1156 15th St. NW, Suite 700, Washington, DC 20005
(202) 973-3000 • fax: (202) 973-3096
e-mail: naral@naral.org • website: www.naral.org

NARAL works to develop and sustain a pro-choice political constituency in order to maintain the right of all women to legal abortion. The league briefs members of Congress and testifies at hearings on abortion and related issues. It publishes the quarterly *NARAL Newsletter.*

National Conference of Catholic Bishops (NCCB)
3211 Fourth St. NE, Washington, DC 20017-1194
(202) 541-3000 • fax: (202) 541-3054
website: www.nccbusc.org

The NCCB, which adheres to the Vatican's opposition to abortion, is the American Roman Catholic bishops' organ for unified action. Through its committee on pro-life activities, it advocates a legislative ban on abortion and promotes state restrictions on abortion, such as parental consent/notification laws and strict licensing laws for abortion clinics. Its pro-life publications include the educational kit *Respect Life* and the monthly newsletter *Life Insight.*

National Right to Life Committee (NRLC)
419 Seventh St. NW, Suite 500, Washington, DC 20004
(202) 626-8800
e-mail: nrlc@nrlc.org • website: www.nrlc.org

NRLC is one of the largest organizations opposing abortion. The committee campaigns against legislation to legalize abortion. It encourages ratification of a constitutional amendment granting embryos and fetuses the same right to life as living persons, and it advocates alternatives to abortion, such as adoption. NRLC publishes the brochure *When Does Life Begin?* and the *National Right to Life News.*

Planned Parenthood Federation of America (PPFA)
810 Seventh Ave., New York, NY 10019
(212) 541-7800 • fax: (212) 245-1845
e-mail: communications@ppfa.org • website: www.plannedparenthood.org

PPFA is a national organization that supports people's right to make their own reproductive decisions without governmental interference. It provides contraception, abortion, and family planning services at clinics located throughout the United States. Among its extensive publications are the pamphlets *Abortions: Questions and Answers, Five Ways to Prevent Abortion,* and *Nine Reasons Why Abortions Are Legal.*

Religious Coalition for Reproductive Choice (RCRC)
1025 Vermont Ave. NW, Suite 1130, Washington, DC 20005
(202) 628-7700 • fax: (202) 628-7716
e-mail: info@rcrc.org • website: www.rcrc.org

RCRC consists of more than thirty Christian, Jewish, and other religious groups committed to helping individuals to make decisions concerning abortion in accordance with their conscience. The organization supports abortion rights, opposes antiabortion violence, and educates policy makers and the public about the diversity of religious perspectives on abortion. RCRC publishes booklets, an educational essay series, the pamphlets *Abortion and the Holocaust: Twisting the Language* and *Judaism and Abortion,* and the quarterly *Religious Coalition for Reproductive Choice Newsletter.*

Bibliography

Books

Mary Boyle
Re-Thinking Abortion: Psychology, Gender, Power, and the Law. London: Routledge, 1997.

Kimberly J. Cook
Divided Passions: Public Opinions on Abortion and the Death Penalty. Boston: Northeastern University Press, 1998.

Susan Dwyer and Joel Feinburg, eds.
The Problem of Abortion. Belmont, CA: Wadsworth, 1997.

Patrick Lee
Abortion and Unborn Human Life. Washington, DC: Catholic University of America Press, 1996.

Eileen L. McDonagh
Breaking the Abortion Deadlock: From Choice to Consent. New York: Oxford University Press, 1996.

Suzanne T. Poppema with Mike Henderson
Why I Am an Abortion Doctor. Amherst, NY: Prometheus, 1996.

James Risen and July L. Thomas
Wrath of Angels: The American Abortion War. New York: BasicBooks, 1998.

Rickie Solinger, ed.
Abortion Wars: A Half Century of Struggle, 1950–2000. Berkeley: University of California Press, 1998.

Raymond Tatalovich
The Politics of Abortion in the United States and Canada: A Comparative Study. Armonk, NY: M.E. Sharpe, 1997.

Michael Thomson
Reproducing Narrative: Gender, Reproduction, and Law. Brookfield, VT: Ashgate, 1998.

Kevin Wm. Wildes and Alan C. Mitchell, eds.
Choosing Life: A Dialogue on Evangelium Vitae. Washington, DC: Georgetown University Press, 1997.

Periodicals

Tony Blankley
"The Fountain of Youth? Moral Dilemmas of Embryo Research," *Washington Times,* April 26, 2000.

Brian A. Brown
"All Too Human," *American Spectator,* July 1999.

Harold O.J. Brown
"Fighting Words: Abortion and Civility," *Chronicles,* August 1998.

Charles Colson and Nancy Pearcey
"Why Max Deserves a Life," *Christianity Today,* June 16, 1997.

Melanie Conklin
"Blocking Women's Health Care," *Progressive,* January 1998.

Gregg L. Cunningham
"Wave of the Future?" *National Review,* November 10, 1997.

Gregg Easterbrook   "Abortion and Brain Waves," *New Republic,* January 31, 2000.

Deal W. Hudson   "Stem Cells Equal Baby Parts," *Crisis,* May 2000.

Roger Mahony   " 'Choosing' Not to Say What They Mean: Politicians Use a Ubiquitous Platitude to Avoid Saying That They Support a Politically Correct Moral Evil," *Los Angeles Times,* May 18, 2000.

Betty McCollister   "Four Fallacies in 'Pro-Life' Arguments," *Human Quest,* March/April 2000.

Peggy Noonan   "Abortion's Children," *New York Times,* January 22, 1998.

Katha Pollitt   "Anti-Choice, Anti-Child," *Nation,* November 15, 1999.

David Shenk   "Biocapitalism: What Price the Genetic Revolution?" *Harper's Magazine,* December 1997.

John M. Swomley   "Abortion as a Positive Moral Choice," *Human Quest,* July/August 1999.

Index